Mr Hitchcock

Mr Hitchcock

Quentin Falk

HAUS PUBLISHING • LONDON

Copyright © 2007 Quentin Falk

First published in Great Britain in 2007 by Haus Publishing,
26 Cadogan Court, Draycott Avenue, London SW3 3BX
www.hauspublishing.co.uk

The moral rights of the author have been asserted

A CIP catalogue record for this book is available from the British Library

ISBN 978-1-904950-75-2

Typeset in Adobe Garamond Pro by MacGuru Limited
Printed and bound by Graphicom in Vicenza, Italy
Jacket illustrations: *front* courtesy Topham Picturepoint; *back* akg-Images

For Brian, Stanley, Pruella, Rosie, Neville, Tommy and Beyoncé

Contents

Introduction & Acknowledgements

More than a quarter of a century after his death in 1980, Alfred Hitchcock remains perhaps the most visually quoted of all directors in the history of cinema. This is hardly surprising given, for example, film writer Tom Shone's recent analysis that Hitchcock is 'easily the most modern of directors from Hollywood's mature Golden Age'. While other great directors like Ford and Welles 'seem thoroughly of their time,' Shone asserts perceptively, 'Hitchcock seems like a man who stopped making movies yesterday.' His films have been re-made either directly, or with just the name changed, by countless other important film-makers – like Polanski, De Palma, Schrader and Demme – who would, nevertheless, still be delighted to have the adjective 'Hitchcockian' ascribed to their efforts even if the results are, more often than not, simply pale reflections of an altogether more memorable original. One should also note the arrival in 2006 of *Gas*, a very stylish short film adapted by writer-director Sylvie Bolioli from Hitchcock's own, Poe-inspired, eponymous short story written 90 years ago for the staff magazine of the company where he worked as a technical clerk before entering the film industry a year later.

Millions of words, both accurate and scurrilously speculative, have already been written about the so-called 'Master of Suspense', noting everything from his alleged obsessions with food, murder and idealised love to a fascination with blondes and a love-hate relationship with his own barrel-shaped figure. 'I am,' he once said wittily, 'an expert on losing weight. I have lost hundreds of pounds in my lifetime, and I represent the survival of the fattest … I never achieved the body I wanted, but I am proud of my body of work. It is tall, thin and handsome.' He was married to the same woman for 54 years but supposedly celibate for more than 40 years. He was the first director, British or otherwise, to be his own best publicist and after arriving in Hollywood shortly before the outbreak of the Second World War, was from *Spellbound* (1945) onwards, firmly above-the-title. He was arguably as much – in his own mind, possibly more than – the star of his films as some of the equally great names who graced his casts down the years.

While I didn't expect to come up with anything startlingly new in terms of original research, this new biography hopefully draws together the many strands of his life and career, some of which may have been tucked away into film history's nooks and crannies. My opening chapter contains fresh – in the odd case, first published – interviews with some of Hitchcock's most valued collaborators on a film that contains many of the recurring motifs in his 50-year film-making span. This assignment not only afforded me the chance to catch up with wonderful technicians, some of whom now well into their nineties, but also to re-view a body of work – including recently released DVDs of his silent titles – which, with only very few exceptions, triumphantly stands the test of time.

Thank you to the following for their help and recall: Richard

(Lord) Attenborough, BAFTA (Doreen Dean), Sylvie Bolioli, Anwar Brett, Colin Brewer, Al Clark, Ben Falk, Jon Finch, Bryan Forbes CBE, Peter Handford, David Harcourt, Bryan Langley BSC, Alec McCowen, John Kennedy Melling, John Millar, The National Army Museum (Michael Ball), Optimum Releasing, George Perry, Hugh Stewart, Gilbert Taylor BSC, and Paul Wilson FBKS BSC.

Picture Sources

The author and publishers wish to express their thanks to the following sources of illustrative material and/or permission to reproduce it. They will make proper acknowledgments in future editions in the event that any omissions have occurred.

akg-Images: pp. 5, 24, 33, 81, 117, 119, 132, 137, 140, 147, 149, 152, 154, 159, 163, 166, 171, 173, 177; author's collection: 11; Getty Images: pp. 18, 27, 28, 35, 44, 51, 60, 64, 69, 70, 73, 79, 89, 93, 97, 98, 105, 107, 110, 121, 127, 131, 142; Topham Picturepoint: pp. 58, 64, 125, 169.

Chapter 1

'Maybe it's because I'm a Londoner'

At the turn of the 1970s, when he had himself just turned 70, Alfred Hitchcock was, professionally, at his lowest ebb in an otherwise long and often brilliant career that had started 50 years earlier in the embryo British Film Industry. Although still a household name and face, probably cinema's only superstar director at the time, he actually hadn't had a big hit since *Psycho* in 1960. Since then the frequency of his films had diminished dramatically in direct relation to the box office fortunes of that increasingly meagre output. *Topaz*, his 51st and latest film, had just bombed spectacularly and at a time when, with hit films like *Easy Rider*, Hollywood was beginning to worship at the fountain of youth, Hitchcock, for all his celebrity, must have seemed positively Jurassic in that climate. Of his fellow Victorian-born, A-list film-makers still alive – like John Ford, Mervyn LeRoy, Frank Capra, Raoul Walsh, King Vidor and William Dieterle – only he and George Cukor, who was also born in 1899, were still working. Technically. Of course he didn't really need to work. The profits

from his films and his eponymous television series had made him fabulously well-off with homes in Hollywood, where he'd been resident since 1939, and up the Californian coast. Married to his beloved Alma for more than 40 years, he was also a grandfather of three. Yet the hunger for work – as well as for food, drink and the other good things of life – was still there.

All kinds of international awards and honours had been lavished on him – an Honorary Oscar here, a Chevalier de la Lègion d'honneur there, gala seasons of his films everywhere. Only his native Britain had been tardy with any recognition – official or otherwise – but that was about to change when, in March 1971, Hitchcock was invited to the Royal Albert Hall to receive the first ever Fellowship from the Society of Film And Television Arts, BAFTA's predecessor. Richard Attenborough, who was the chairman of the Society at the time and the host of the event, outlined the enormity of the award to the 1,400 guests in a place which, coincidentally Hitchcock had used so spectacularly for both versions of *The Man Who Knew Too Much*, in 1934 and 1956.

'One of the most important milestones in the history of the Society …' intoned Attenborough, ' … someone who has created work in film and TV that has made a lasting impact on all of us in this industry … to a man who has entertained us, made us smile, made us worry and perhaps even sometimes terrified us …' Then, following clips from *Psycho*, *Saboteur*, *Shadow of a Doubt*, *Spellbound* and *North by Northwest*, the man himself rose from a table at the front of the hall and waddled, a little gingerly, up on stage to the predictable accompaniment of his 'dum-di diddly dun-di-da' TV theme and an equally predictable standing ovation. As he received a statuette and scroll from the Society's President, HRH Princess Anne, Hitchcock could be seen mouthing a polite 'Thank you!' while, also politely, he shook the royal hand. Then it was to centre stage where, in front of the microphone, he speechified slowly and with admirable straight face: 'I am deeply honoured, of course, to receive this from my fellow technicians. I was a technician in England I think as far back as

1920 … and I behaved myself ever since [laughter and applause]. Rather recently, I was recipient of a very important honour by the French government and it made me very very appreciative. I asked if it could be presented by M Henri Langlois, head of the Cinematheque Française, probably the greatest French museum in the world. He was, if I may say so, a man of some proportions [laughter] and we met and I think he just about made the presentation – but there is one difference. That night, he did kiss me on both cheeks!' Cue Hitchcock music as he left the stage to yet more laughter and rapturous applause. Although the British industry had now done its stuff, the reference to state-sponsored Gallic appreciation certainly wasn't lost on the crowd. That kind of domestic recognition would only arrive shortly before his death nine years later.

All kinds of memories must surely have flooded back as he sat that evening in the Royal Albert Hall, not just of those two films directly connected with the place but also of his childhood in East London and exciting formative years in the UK industry. In fact, the trip back to collect his Fellowship would be just the beginning of an almost year-long, often nostalgic, delve into his indigenous past. After the costly *Topaz*, Hitchcock must have wondered how supportive Universal Pictures, to whom he'd been contracted since *The Birds* in 1962, would be of future projects. As with so many of the director's other films, the roots of what was to be his penultimate movie also went back some years, in this case to an idea he'd worked on, first with Benn Levy then Howard Fast, about a brutal serial killer. And that's all it had remained, an idea, while he directed *Torn Curtain* then *Topaz* before being given a copy of Arthur La Bern's 1966 potboiler, *Goodbye Piccadilly, Farewell Leicester Square*. La Bern's lurid, London-set cat-and-mouse rape-murder plot – with its interweaving tale of psychotic sex murderer and a rather seedy ex-serviceman accused of the crimes – seemed to chime perfectly with Hitchcock's outline idea for something always to have been called – the title seemed all-important to him – *Frenzy*. Although Universal were clearly not prepared to sanction another expensive international film like *Topaz* again, especially without stars, they were open to Hitchcock's persuasion to back a more modestly budgeted film (at $2 million, half the cost of *Topaz*), to be shot in England with a cast of hand-picked, experienced theatre professionals.

It had been more than 20 years since Hitchcock last shot an entire film in his native country and he probably thought that this might now be a rather belated chance towards the end of his career to try and recreate a fast and furious thriller along the same lines as some of his more breathless British films of the 1930s. There was one big difference, though, according to Anthony Shaffer who was recruited by Hitchcock to write the screenplay: the director wanted to be more explicit and violent than ever before. Shaffer, who'd just had a big stage hit with *Sleuth*, was contacted by Hitchcock on New Year's Eve, 1970, and at first thought it was a hoax. When the arrival of La Bern's book followed the call, he was convinced and set about the task with relish. Aside from its familiar Hitchcockian theme of the innocent man digging himself deeper into distress, the director's principal filmic interest in an otherwise rather unappetising book appeared to revolve around one particularly macabre scene. This involved the killer bundling one of his victims into the back of a long-distance potato lorry so that the body would eventually be discovered far away from the scene of the crime. When he suddenly realises that she's still grasping the key to his London flat, he has to try and remove the incriminating evidence while in transit from a body beginning to go into rigor among large sacks of spuds. The combination of these elements and a chance also to re-visit and recreate Covent Garden (then due for imminent demolition and relocation), a big part of the Hitchcock family history, was clearly irresistible.

For what Hitchcock's authorised biographer, John Russell Taylor, described as his 'triumphal return' to England, the film-maker established three bases of operation during the preparation and production of *Frenzy*: at the company office in Piccadilly, Pinewood Studios and in his lavish suite at Claridge's. Although there were one or two regular Hitchcock collaborators on the strength like long-time assistant Peggy Robertson and effects man Albert Whitlock, the recruiting of cast and crew proved to be a mixture of brand new and the odd rather poignant re-union. Cinematographer Gil Taylor had been an 18-year-old camera assistant when he last worked with Hitchcock on *Number Seventeen* in 1932, the same year actress Elsie Randolph – here as a hall porteress – had previously emoted for the director in *Rich and Strange*. Taylor finally got a chance to confess that it had been him who had all those years earlier snipped Hitchcock's tie in the darkroom, giving him a taste of his own inexhaustible practical joking medicine. This, Taylor recalled, also extended to slipping Ex-Lax in technicians' coffee then locking the stage doors for hours on end to observe their increasing discomfort. Sound man Peter Handford's 'previous' didn't go back quite as far – only to *Under Capricorn* in 1949 and would have continued a year later on *Stage Fright*, Hitchcock's last film in England, had he not already been contracted to MGM at the time. Never one to duck a bit of mischief-making, Hitchcock, said Handford, invited him to lunch at Associated British's Elstree Studios under the very noses of the local union people who'd threatened they would strike if the recordist was employed on that film.

Like Shaffer, Alec McCowen could hardly believe it when his agent rang to say that Hitchcock wanted him to play the part of the detective, Chief Inspector Oxford, and to meet the director in Piccadilly. 'I found myself chatting to him for about half an hour assuming I wouldn't get the part. I was already a huge fan and wanted to ask him about various great moments in his films – like the Westminster Cathedral scene in *Foreign Correspondent*, Mount Rushmore in *North by Northwest* and climbing over the Statue of Liberty in *Saboteur*. He loved to talk about them and I don't think *Frenzy* was mentioned at all. We said goodbye and I thought that was it. Then my agent rang again and said he wanted me to do the role. Naturally, I was absolutely thrilled.' Barry Foster, who played the 'Neck Tie Killer' Bob Rusk, had always assumed he was first summoned to the presence as a result of Hitchcock seeing him in David Mercer's play *After Hagerty* in which he co-starred with another of *Frenzy*'s actors, Billie Whitelaw. He later learned that it was actually because of his performance in the Boultings' 1968 thriller, *Twisted Nerve*, which had been roundly described by critics as having a 'Hitchcock flavour'. In fact, first choice for the role had been Michael Caine who revealed in his autobiography, *What's It All About?*, that, despite his admiration for the 'great man', he found the part 'really loathsome and I did not want to be associated with it … The only thing I can remember about our lunch was plucking up enough courage to ask him if he had, as reported, said that actors were cattle. "No," he said with a smile. "What I actually said was that they should be treated like cattle which, you must agree, Michael, is an entirely different thing."' Jon Finch had just finished filming the title role of *Macbeth* for Polanski when he was perfunctorily auditioned for the role of down-on-his-luck ex-flier Richard Blaney who seems to be taking the rap for his old friend, Rusk. Although invited to view footage of *Macbeth*, Hitchcock declined and watched instead some old black-and-white TV work of Finch after which they met. Said Finch: 'I was already half in shock from seeing the man. He told me he'd seen some film of me. "You can act which is good. Would you like to do it?" I said yes and he replied, "Good – let's go and have lunch." That was it.'

Anna Massey originally went up for the part of Monica, a snooty secretary (eventually played by Jean Marsh) but actually landed the meatier assignment of doomed barmaid Babs Milligan

Barry Foster and Alec McCowen take direction from the master on the set of **Frenzy,** *1971*

who ends up in the potato sack. Unlike Barbara Leigh Hunt, playing the film's first victim, Blaney's ex-wife Brenda, who told Hitchcock that she wouldn't contemplate any nudity (and had a clause in her contract to that effect), Massey always assumed from the script that she would be required to strip. In the event, body doubles were used for both actresses. Once cast, Hitchcock just expected his actors to do a professional job, hit their marks and perform the lines pretty much as written. As filming finally got underway in the summer of 1971, Jon Finch began to make it pretty clear he was less than enamoured with Shaffer's script. Another Hitchcock first-timer and his strong right arm was First Assistant Director Colin Brewer, who'd previously worked with John Huston and Carol Reed. Brewer recalled: 'Finch was rather full of himself and one day on the stage at Pinewood said to Hitch, "I don't like the dialogue in this scene". Everything went very quiet. Hitch just said, "Put the lights out, Colin. Get one of your assistants on the phone to contact Mr Shaffer and tell him that Jon Finch doesn't like his dialogue." Now it went deathly silent. I did as I was told and my assistant had got as far as talking to Shaffer when Finch then said, "I'm terribly sorry, Mr Hitchcock." Said Hitch, "Now we'll shoot the scene Mr Shaffer's way."'

Alec McCowen got the sense that Hitchcock wasn't that interested in the dialogue scenes saving all his energy and focus instead for what would be his latest pieces of trademark action. Which didn't mean he neglected the actors altogether, as McCowen discovered. 'At the Old Bailey scene when we'd sent the wrong man to prison, I had this big close up. Hitch spent a great deal of time of that, explaining to me, "we want to know what's in your eyes. It's halfway through the film and the audience have to be riveted as to what's going to happen next, and it's all in your face." He took that shot over and over again. Then it came to the end of the film when I make the final arrest and I have to say to Rusk, "You're not wearing your necktie …" I felt a bit like Kirk Douglas or something and came on to do that line very tough as I thought that was the right way to play it. Hitchcock stopped me and said, "You know, Alec, if I was playing your part which I'm not, I wouldn't come on all tough like that. It's the end of the film, you've got your man. I might say it quite quietly; I might sigh, laugh even – but I wouldn't come on all tough. But it's up to you – you're playing the part." Of course, I tried to do it *his* way.'

Like many of the other cast and crew, McCowen and especially Peter Handford felt that for Hitchcock, actually making the film was at times a rather boring interruption in between catching up on his past, telling colourful anecdotes and enjoying copious amounts of food, wine and, during shooting, vodka and orange, which he'd swig slyly. Everything had been already worked out in his mind; committing it to film was, frankly, dull and, after a large lunch every day, increasingly a serious chore. Said Brewer: 'We'd be doing a scene and I'd look round for the "Cut!" and he was asleep in his chair. So I'd say "Cut!" at which point he'd wake up and he'd say, "What are you doing?". I'd reply "Shot it, Hitch" to which he'd say, "How was it for you, old bean?" I never quite knew what to say to that but generally replied, "Fine, Hitch". To which he'd then usually say, "OK, print it." There were also times when I would have to tell him we were getting a bit behind schedule, so one day we simply shot 10 pages when the normal was three. "There you are, old bean. Now we're back on schedule," he'd laugh.' McCowen remembered one particular occasion when Hitchcock was aroused from his post-lunch slumber with Brewer saying, 'Hitch, would you like to see that again?' To which the director replied, 'Yes – and tell them to do it louder!' Clad every day in his perennial dark blue suit, white shirt and blue tie, he only socialised with the actors in the sense that, as McCowen said, 'he loved to talk'. After arriving at Pinewood from Claridge's in his Rolls-Royce, he'd hold court early each morning: 'He'd often give us a little cabaret of memories for maybe three-quarters of an hour and then shout, with a smile, "Why are we wasting time?"'

Hitchcock's interest in the film only properly perked up with the planning and, in most cases, the execution of his trademark set-pieces. One of the more memorable is when Rusk leads Babs up the stairs to his Covent Garden flat where we know he's going to kill her. Just outside and then inside the building the soundtrack becomes eerily silent with the quietude only briefly broken as Rusk utters his murderous pre-amble, 'You're my kind of woman'. The camera then leaves them at the door at the top of the stairs before retreating back down the stairs and out into a suddenly noisy, bustling street. Gil Taylor and his camera operator Paul Wilson both knew that Hitchcock revelled in this kind of visual challenge. His knowledge of lenses remained peerless while his trust in his collaborators to achieve the effect was absolute. He had, said Taylor, never felt the need to look through the camera himself perhaps ever since his first great cameraman Jack Cox had told him to 'take your bleedin' eye away from that – that's my job.' On *Frenzy*, Taylor claimed, Hitchcock didn't even bother to go to rushes for the first three weeks of shooting, adding, 'I made him go because we weren't sure if we'd suddenly all get the sack if he didn't like what he'd seen.' As the sequence that had, initially, most piqued his interest, Hitchcock quite rigorously storyboarded the body-and-potatoes episode with a tiepin now substituted for the key. But when it came to the night shooting of the scene, he was, on that occasion, rather more pre-occupied with a couple of Royal visitors to the set – his former star Princess

14

Grace [Kelly] and her husband Prince Rainier. 'You can finish the night,' he told Colin Brewer, before heading out to dinner with his old friends. That wasn't the first or last piece of directing undertaken on the film by the First AD. One of Brewer's most precious keepsakes from that time is a framed photograph of him and Hitchcock, signed by Hitchcock thus: 'The Director and his assistant (on the left).' Hitchcock was, of course, pictured to the left. Brewer's other reward was sole screen credit.

The film's most problematic scene, and the one that in a way sums up the strange, often uncomfortable nature of this whole enterprise that generally fails to reconcile its 1950s-type plot with a 1970s morality, is the unpleasantly prolonged rape-murder of Brenda Blaney. It was bad enough for the actors, Barry Foster and Barbara Leigh Hunt, who spent three days shooting it. And it might have looked even worse in the final version had Hitchcock got his way. He wanted an extreme close up of her in death with her tongue sticking out through saliva and blood. Anthony Shaffer saw that shot in the rushes and pleaded with Hitchcock to remove it because it was, well, 'disgusting'. Hitchcock replied he couldn't see a problem but by the time of the second assembly of the negative, Shaffer was gratified to notice the shot had been deleted. It's certainly not difficult to see why Jon Finch had difficulty with the script. Aside from the odd shaft of black comedy and some fun with the Inspector having to deal with his wife's increasingly unappetising attempts at gourmet cooking, the dialogue veers unevenly between 'gor blimey', stiff-upper-lip and modishly foul-mouthed. The novel had dealt with middle-aged relics from the Second World War; the film could plead no such excuses with ghastly 1970s clothes and hairstyles betraying a cast who'd have been far too young anyway for such a conflict. If parts of the screenplay appeared simply dated, then some others

'A third assistant director came up to me and said, "Mr Hitchcock wants to see you in his caravan". I went in there and he had this whole tea service laid out, also cucumber sandwiches and pieces of cake. "Come on, Paul, sit down and have your tea." I said, "But we've a shot to do …" He replied, "Don't worry, Paul, it's only a film. Sit down." He then started asking me about my family, nothing at all to do with the film. He made sure I'd finished my tea before we went back to doing the shot.'
PAUL WILSON

were just unacceptably offensive. 'He rapes them first,' whispers one pub-goer to another. 'Nice to know every cloud has a silver lining,' comes a beyond-the-pale retort. That kind of leering, voyeuristic quality affects the whole film.

Around the film, Hitchcock had a couple of other major problems to deal with, the first of which may have clearly affected his own performance and hastened his increasing torpor. Alma had a minor stroke and the little woman who had been almost constantly by his side since they married in 1926 returned to California for treatment and after-care. Then, in almost a reprise of the situation from *Torn Curtain* when long-time collaborator Bernard Herrmann's music was summarily replaced by John Addison's, Hitchcock decided to re-commission the soundtrack for *Frenzy*. On this occasion, Henry Mancini's music was unceremoniously dumped in favour of a jaunty new score by Ron Goodwin, as British as Bow Bells.

When Hitchcock returned to London the following May for the World Premiere, where he asked for members of his crew to flank him and the now-recovered Alma, he might have reasonably expected the worst – the final sealing of a hat-trick of box-office disasters. Almost against the odds, some might suggest quite unaccountably, the reviews were incredibly respectful at worst and ecstatic at best – 'A psychological thriller that ranks among his very best and shows the 72-year-old director in triumphant command of his unmatched artistic powers', lauded *Newsweek*. A *succès d'estime*, as his French fans might say, was one thing, a financial winner can be quite another. Yet, it soon became clear that one would follow the other and the film went on to gross more than $16 million. After more than 40 years at the top of his profession, Hitchcock's reputation was, like his egg-shaped physique, now weightier than ever.

Chapter 2

High road to Islington

A blue plaque proclaims the following: 'Alfred Joseph Hitchcock. The famous film director was born near this site at 517 High Road Leytonstone on August 13th 1899. Died April 24th 1980.' It would be good to report that this pithy information about unarguably Britain's most famous filmmaker is to be found in some suitably elegant and properly prominent corner of the East London borough that was, in his day, part of the county of Essex. In fact, it is actually located halfway up a boring red-brick wall at the rear of a Jet petrol station between the office and a garish eatery next door called 'Chick's Chicken And Pizza'. Another notice, declaring 'Switch Turn Off Petrol Pumps Here' competes with Hitchcock's Heritage plaque for your attention in this dimly-lit backwater.

Not that that the area isn't truly proud of its most famous son. At Leytonstone tube station – not to be confused with nearby mainline Leytonstone High Road station, which opened for business five years before Hitchcock was born – there's an astonishing permanent tribute to celebrate the centenary of his birth. Commissioned in 1999 and unveiled two years later, it comprises,

John Stuart and Leon M Lion looking like caricature villains in Hitchcock's film Number Seventeen, *a thriller about a gang of jewel thieves, 1932*

following local consultation, a series of 17 mosaics, specifically scenes from 14 of his films including automatic choices such as *Psycho*, *North By Northwest* and *The Birds* as well as rather less obvious titles like *Number Seventeen* and *The Wrong Man*. In addition there are three depictions of Hitchcock on and off set: one of him as a child on horseback, as a director on *The Skin Game* (albeit with a fantasy cast of Margaret Lockwood, Peter Lorre and Ingrid Bergman) and of him and Marlene Dietrich on a sofa. However, artistic licence seems to have completely run riot with sights of Leytonstone appearing inexplicably in the mosaics of *Rebecca* (St John's Church), *Saboteur* (the High Road) and *Rear Window* (The Green Man public house).

There is also, happily, a depiction of 517 High Road where Hitchcock arrived in this world as the third child – following William and Nellie, respectively nine and seven years his senior – of William and Emma who were married in 1886 in the final quarter of Queen Victoria's long reign. They lived literally above the shop, a greengrocer's, but that rather modest term doesn't quite convey the full extent of William Sr's burgeoning business. As well as retail he also supplied wholesale fruit and veg to various other local outlets and would eventually join forces with his three brothers, who were all fishmongers, to create a chain (later the cornerstone of the Mac Fisheries empire) throughout South London.

The hardworking Hitchcocks, clearly lower middle-class pillars of the local neighbourhood, were both practising Catholics, which meant that their youngest child made a very early acquaintance with Church and Sunday School. His father was also, by all accounts, a strict man not averse to giving his children the occasional short, sharp shock. Alfred was apparently only five when, following some mild domestic misdeed, he was famously – maybe even apocryphally – dispatched to the local police station with a note from his father. After reading the missive, the officer on duty allegedly locked the little boy in a cell for five minutes telling him, 'this is what we do to naughty boys'. Judging by his regular, animated re-telling of this childhood incident, the effect was profound and, he would claim, engendered in him a lifelong fear of the police.

One can easily imagine an impression of this vivid tableau in the mosaic homage but neither that nor perhaps some indication of an early brush with the art form, which would make his fame and fortune, made it into the final selection. Cinema was, of course, still in its infancy when Hitchcock was born. As far as the general public was concerned, pictures first officially moved in 1895 when on 28 December that year the Lumière Brothers terrified a Paris audience with flickering scenes of a train hurtling towards them. Recorded by the brothers during their family holiday in July the same year, the innocent-sounding footage billed as *L'Arrivé d'un Train en Gare* caused a sensation with audience members ducking behind their seats, convinced that the engine was about to run over them. For the price of one franc each, the Parisians had in effect witnessed the first screen 'monster'.

There is no record of whether Hitchcock, who in later years would undoubtedly have approved of this extreme audience reaction, ever got to see what is often regarded as the first ever horror film. From his teens, however, he was a self-confessed film buff: 'Though I went to the theatre very often, I preferred the movies and was more attracted to American films than the British. I saw pictures of Chaplin, Griffith, all the Paramount Famous Players pictures, Buster Keaton, Douglas Fairbanks, Mary Pickford, as well as the German films of Decla-Bioscop, the company that preceded UFA.'[1] Griffith's successive epics *Birth of a Nation* (1915) and *Intolerance* (1916) seemed to have made a particular impression. Hitchcock would eventually go on record with 'like all directors, I was influenced by Griffith'.[2]

By the time he fell seriously in love with cinema, which was accompanied by an equal passion for the UK film trade journals of the day – like *Kinematograph Weekly* and *Bioscope* – he'd also undergone a serious Catholic education. Soon after the family moved to Poplar in 1907 to accommodate an enlargement of the business, Hitchcock was enrolled at the Howrah House Convent. Then, two years later, after yet another house move, this time to Stepney (and a short, unhappy stint as a boarder at the Salesian College in Battersea) he started as a day boy (later a boarder) aged 11 at the formidable Jesuit-run St Ignatius College in Stamford Hill, about a three-mile bus ride north of the East End. 'It was probably during this period with the Jesuits that a strong sense of fear developed – moral fear – the fear of being involved in anything evil. I always tried to avoid it. Why? Perhaps out of physical fear. I was terrified of physical punishment.'[3] The threat of a hard rubber cane seemed to concentrate the mind wonderfully, if a little fearfully, over the next four years as Hitchcock proved a just-about-above-average student enjoying English literature, geography and even the occasional school prize.

Far younger than his siblings, generally a bit of a loner and hardly blessed with good looks, he also began to develop a fertile imagination fuelled by an almost obsessive interest in bus and rail timetables. By the age of 16, 'he knew the geography of New York by heart from maps … and he prided himself on being able to recite from memory all the stops on the Orient Express.' [4] As well as planning imaginary journeys – ways of escape? – for which he'd often draw his own maps, real and imagined, there was also an early fascination with crime and he'd take himself off to the Old Bailey and watch trials.

Trying to pin down the precise chronology of these hobbies, which seemed to have alternated with solo theatre and cinema-going, proves to be as tricky as ascertaining the exact sequence of events involving his father's untimely death at 52 in December 1914 and Hitchcock's departure from St Ignatius. According to at least one major biographer he left the College in July 1913 and was then, aged 14, encouraged by his parents to attend some evening lectures in navigation at London University. There is, however, a severe discrepancy between this and other, arguably more authoritative, accounts which suggest that he was still at St Ignatius' when, more than a year later, he was summoned home to be told about the death of his father. These, including Hitchcock's own recollection (except that he suggests *both* his parents were alive at the time and probably resident back in Leytonstone), then go on to relate that he went, briefly, to the School of Engineering and Navigation in nearby Poplar. What is certain is that, four months before William Sr succumbed of a combination of chronic emphysema and kidney disease, Britain had declared war on Germany.

With no suggestion that he was to follow his brother into the family business, Hitchcock had, at 15, a living to earn. Armed with some specialised training in mechanics, electricity, acoustics and, of course, navigation, he got a job as a technical clerk with the long-established WT Henley Telegraph Company, which made electrical cable. Taking night classes at London University in subjects ranging from economics to drawing, he then progressed at Henley's to estimating clerk and eventually into the advertising department. There, he was able to parlay his increasingly deft skills as a caricaturist into 'writing or editing the copy for newspapers and magazine advertisements and brochures and, more importantly, for laying them out and supplying any graphic illustrations required'.[6]

Meanwhile, as the Great War raged on with increasing slaughter and despair across the Channel about 165 miles to the East of London – with merely the odd air-raid disturbing the peace of the capital – 5ft 7in tall Hitchcock, increasingly rotund if still well short of the mighty 21 stone he'd attain by the mid-1930s, attended his army medical in 1917, was classified C3 and excused active service. Category 'C', which referred to men 'free from serious organic disease, but only able to stand service conditions in garrisons at home', was further subdivided thrice of which '3' required 'sedentary work: for example clerks, storemen, batmen, cooks, orderlies, sanitary duties'. He did however enlist in the volunteer corps of the Royal Engineers, which proved to be more social than practical despite the occasional field exercise in Hyde Park.

A year after peace finally broke out – by which time British film-making had almost ground to a halt – Hitchcock was reading one of his beloved film trades when he noticed a story detailing the plans of the American-based Famous Players-Lasky Company (later to become Paramount Pictures) to open a UK 'arm'. They'd acquired a former railway power station in Poole Street, Islington and were going to convert it into a two-stage film studio with workshops and offices. The story also gave some details of their proposed production schedule, which included a new film version of Marie Corelli's 1895 novel, *The Sorrows of Satan*, which had already been filmed once before (with Gladys Cooper) in 1917. This news galvanised Hitchcock who interpreted the company's future plans as his own chance of a proper entrée into an industry with which, even as an outsider, he was already, he reckoned, quite familiar. Using his increasing drawing/design know-how, he created a series of elaborate title cards – for the captions covering the silent picture dialogue – and hand-delivered them

to Poole Street, only to be informed that the Corelli project had been abandoned. Instead, the company had decided to adapt Louis N Parker and George Sims' play, *The Great Day*, a drama with echoes of the First World War, as their inaugural British production. Undaunted, Hitchcock fashioned a new series of title cards overnight and went back to Islington the following day.

Not unnaturally, Famous Players-Lasky were 'sufficiently impressed, by his persistence if not by his art, to give him some work, which he did moonlighting from Henley's – an arrangement his immediate superior agreed to on one condition – that they split the profits 50-50.'[7] Not long after that, the film company offered the 20-year-old a full-time job and for the next three years he designed the title cards for all of their output, some 11 films in all, including *The Call of Youth*, *The Man from Home* (starring the statuesque Swedish import, Anna Q Nilsson), and *Spanish Jade*, with Evelyn Brent, one of Hollywood's finest. Describing himself by this stage as 'very fat and very ambitious',[8] it seemed only a matter of time before he would, in this distinctly free-wheeling industry, actually get a chance to direct for what 'the young Hitchcock had brought home to him was the degree to which one could lie with pictures, or re-arrange and re-interpret them to make them signify almost anything you wanted them to … the film-maker was sovereign in his own little world, the world he created first by shooting the film and then, even more decisively, by fiddling about with the pieces, laying them end to end first this way and then that.'[9]

The chance came as early as 1922 when, following a falling-out at the studio between writer-director Hugh Croise and producer-star Seymour Hicks, the handily-placed Hitchcock was invited by the actor-manager to complete his short, *Always Tell Your Wife*, a remake of the same comedy Hicks had first filmed with his wife, Ellaline Terriss, back in 1914. Hitchcock was uncredited for the work but struck up enough of a rapport with Hicks to be asked to direct his next film, another two-reeler, *Number 13* (also known as *Mrs Peabody*). Again Hitchcock would remain uncredited, this time simply because the production ran out of money and was never actually completed. Filming coincided with the decision

by Famous Players-Lasky to pull out of their British commit-
ment (their Islington films hadn't set cinema alight either critically or commercially) and regroup back in the States. In 1924
they finally sold the studio to up-and-coming Birmingham-born
film executive Michael Balcon and his associates. The new entity
would be called Gainsborough Pictures.

Hitchcock had already linked up with Balcon as an assistant
director when the latter, just three years his senior, first became
a tenant at Islington where together with his partners, Victor
Saville and money man John Freedman, they planned to make a
series of films directed by the experienced Graham 'Jack' Cutts.
The first was to be *Woman to Woman*, based on Michael Morton's
stage play, a romantic drama involving amnesia and shell-shock.
Hitchcock had written a script on spec and it was gratefully
accepted by Balcon and Co although his credit was eventually
shared with Cutts. *Woman to Woman* was the first of a series
of features over the next 18 months which would demonstrate
Hitchcock's extreme versatility as he served variously on *The
White Shadow*, *The Passionate Adventure*, *The Blackguard* and *The
Prude's Fall* as writer, art director, production manager and editor
as well as the increasingly jealous Cutts's assistant director.

Hitchcock would later say that *Woman to Woman* was the best
of the bunch but that thought might have been influenced by
the fact he first met his future wife Alma Reville on the film.
Born just a day after him, and as tiny as he was increasingly
barrel-like, she was working in the cutting room and as a script
girl (continuity) at the studio. They were engaged during the
production of *The Prude's Fall* and married the following year,
1926, at Brompton Oratory, by which time Hitchcock had made
his official feature film debut as a director, with Reville (who'd
converted to Catholicism) by his side. *The Pleasure Garden*, based

*Film company partners Victor
Saville, Michael Balcon and Harry
Adley photographed at the house of
the actress Edna Best in 1931*

on a romantic novel by Mrs Oliver Sandys, was to be an Anglo-German co-production filmed on location in Italy and Germany, principally at Munich's Emelka Studios, which proved to be an altogether quieter and more provincial set-up than the great Neubabelsberg Studios – hub of the UFA film-making empire in Berlin – where Hitchcock had previously worked on *The Black-guard* as an assistant. He'd claimed that Balcon's offer of promotion came as a big surprise, that he was perfectly happy writing and art directing and that becoming a director was furthest from his thoughts at that stage. However, Cutts had made it clear he didn't want Hitchcock on his team anymore so Balcon's selection seemed perfectly logical.

From Hitchcock's own colourful tales of the various misadventures that overtook filming – including the confiscation of film stock by Italian customs and the theft of location expenses – he certainly had more than his share of headaches, among them an experienced Hollywood star, Virginia Valli. 'It rained the first day. Then when we started shooting Virginia Valli's scenes, I was in a cold sweat. I wanted to disguise the fact this was my first directorial effort. I dreaded to think what she, an established Hollywood star, would say if she discovered that she had been brought all the way over to Europe to be directed by a beginner. I was terrified at giving her instructions. I've no idea how many times I asked my future wife if I was doing the right thing. She, sweet soul, gave me courage by swearing I was doing marvellously. And Virginia Valli played her scenes sublimely unconscious of the emotional drama that was being enacted on the other side of the camera.'[10]

While the 'prentice Hitchcock was manfully plugging away in Munich with his melodrama of two chorus girls (Valli and Carmelita Geraghty) on the prowl for wealthy husbands, he must have, albeit briefly, thought fondly of his last time in Germany

One of the silent movie era's great heroines, Virginia Valli was the first major star that Hitchcock directed

when he was at least able, from time to time, to infiltrate the masterclass taking place on a neighbouring set at Neubabelsberg. Here, he could observe, at fairly close quarters, the making of a silent screen classic, *The Last Laugh*, F W Murnau's tragic tale, written by Carl Mayer, about the humiliation of an ageing hotel doorman (Emil Jannings). Despite the superficial simplicity of the story, Hitchcock was plainly dazzled by Murnau's style and technical wizardry. Yet, Murnau explained, "'what you can see on the set does not matter. The only truth that counts is what you see on the screen." It was a lesson Hitch was never to forget.'[11]

Balcon would express surprise that, technically, the film looked more American than Continental, while the German producers were rather exercised by a climactic scene of mild brutality involving madness and violent death. Though personally more than happy with his protégé's debut, Balcon was also duty bound to listen to the opinions of his star director and principal money-maker, 'Jack' Cutts. He, for reasons one suspects rather more than just commercial, successfully persuaded the Gainsborough chiefs that *The Pleasure Garden* was likely to be a flop and the film was shelved. By the time it was finally released in 1927, Hitchcock had directed *The Mountain Eagle* – another Anglo-German effort also held until later – and, much more significantly, *The Lodger*, which, as far as the general public were concerned was their first proper encounter with the blossoming 'Master of Suspense'.

Chapter 3

Elstree Calling

One of the films that apparently made a big impression on Hitchcock in his pre-directing days was *Destiny*, Fritz Lang's stylish if eccentric time-jumping, cross-cultural 1921 melodrama. There was, however, no time for sentiment when, as set designer on *The Blackguard*, he successfully ordered – despite UFA's objections – Lang's remarkable forest set at Neubabelsberg for the recently completed *Siegfried* to be torn down to make way for a dream sequence he'd designed and was also going to supervise shooting. Although we know, as previously chronicled, that Hitchcock met Murnau in Berlin, there's a suggestion that he was also able to closely observe Lang at work on his great Expressionist classic *Metropolis* but it is unlikely they actually got together. Film critics would later compare the two directors but, according to Patrick McGilligan's *Fritz Lang*, the German 'detested the comparison, feeling that in the category of thrillers and suspense, the critics tended to favour the upstart Englishman – who, after all, borrowed shamelessly from him'.[12]

However, it's surely reasonable to deduce that not only Murnau but also probably Lang were rather more than just subconscious influences when Hitchcock came to direct *The Lodger*. Subtitled 'A Tale of the London Fog', it was full of 'dark shadows, strange angles and disconcerting compositions in order to convey an atmosphere of neurosis and ambiguity'.[13] The 'first true "Hitchcock movie"',[14] as he described it, it was also the film which first established a series of the film-maker's recurring motifs. Based loosely on the story of Jack the Ripper, the setting is London in the 1920s where a mysterious strangler known as The Avenger leaves his calling card under the skirts of his blonde victims. In this climate of fear and distrust we meet The Lodger who suddenly steps out of the fog looking for a room to rent. Naturally he becomes the prime suspect – for us the audience, and his neighbours. In the original 1913 novel and subsequent stage play, The Lodger did indeed turn out to be the killer, but as Hitchcock had cast 32-year-old matinee idol Ivor Novello as the titular character, the director was soon made aware that the Welshman's legion of fans wouldn't countenance such villainy. So out of commercial necessity was born Hitchcock's oft-repeated plotline of an innocent man in extreme jeopardy. Novello's character is all but lynched before the truth finally comes out which perhaps was some sort of compromise, but Hitchcock's preferred resolution would have been ambiguity: 'in a story of this kind I might have liked him to go off into the night so that we would never really know for sure.'[15]

As well as blondes and endangered innocence, there was the onset of other Hitchcock staples such as dazzling cinematic trickery and, of course, the cameo appearance. Most famously in *The Lodger*, Hitchcock used a glass floor on which Novello would pace back and forth and under which we see his increasingly suspicious boarding-house landlord and family. As a chandelier sways to and fro, the silence is creepily deafening. As for that

cameo, Hitchcock appears not just once but twice – first in a newsroom then as one of a crowd baying for The Lodger's blood – 'it was strictly utilitarian; we had to fill the screen. Later on it became a superstition and eventually a gag albeit', Hitchcock would concede, 'a rather troublesome gag'.[16] The idea would be to get it out of the way in the first five minutes so it wouldn't prove a serious distraction for by-now expectant audiences.

The Lodger eventually proved a huge hit, but not before all

Ivor Novello and June Tripp starred in Hitchcock's first major commercial and critical hit, The Lodger

kinds of hand-wringing by the corporate powers-that-be who, fearing a commercial disaster, put the release of the film firmly on hold. Once again, the chief doomsayer was Cutts who now plainly feared Hitchcock as a usurper. His reservations were however also shared by the distribution company, it seems, so Michael Balcon decided to ask the young critic (later producer) and co-founder of The Film Society, Ivor Montagu, for his independent opinion. A great fan of European cinema, he was immediately bowled over by *The Lodger* and expressed himself forcefully on the matter. More practically he was able to get the ear of Hitchcock and gently suggest some re-editing, the odd bit of re-shooting and, perhaps most intriguingly, to urge the reduction of title cards so that the film would rely more than ever on the purely visual. Hitchcock, happily or pragmatically, went along with all of this. When his beloved *Bioscope* then trumpeted, 'It is possible that this film is the finest British production ever made … a directorial triumph', all the hassle must have seemed worthwhile. On the back of *The Lodger*'s success, both *The Pleasure Garden* and *The Mountain Eagle* finally got released.

At 28, newly-married and living with Alma in a smart flat in Cromwell Road, London SW7, Hitchcock went into overdrive directing in quick succession, *Downhill* and *Easy Virtue*, both edited by Ivor Montagu. Though neither film – the first, starring Ivor Novello in an adaptation of his own stage play, the second from a Noel Coward play – matched *The Lodger* for sheer virtuosity, they continued to enhance Hitchcock's growing reputation. He was also, using an expression that wouldn't properly enter the film industry lexicon for a few more decades, 'bankable'. This was something that obviously immediately struck 52-year-old John Maxwell, the one-time Glasgow solicitor, who, in 1927, set up British International Pictures (BIP) at Elstree followed a

year later by his inauguration of the ABC cinema chain starting with 40 theatres. With the promise of bigger budgets and more freedom, Hitchcock quit Islington for Borehamwood, Herts, and Maxwell's studio – nicknamed 'The Porridge Factory' – on a three-year, 12-picture contract at £13,000 a year. What, incidentally, had become of Cutts by now? As Hitchcock's star rose so his fell almost as rapidly. Within a decade he was even being foisted on Hitchcock as an assistant because Cutts desperately needed the money. Much later, Balcon wrote: 'Hitch could not

Alfred Hitchcock and Alma Reville are showered with confetti on their wedding day, 16 December 1926

35

understand what he had done to offend Cutts; it was only that Cutts was jealous. Hitch was rising too fast for Cutts's taste and he resented him as a rival at the same studio.'[17]

Hitchcock said that after *The Lodger*, *The Ring* – his first project at Elstree – was 'the next Hitchcock picture'.[18] But his own story, co-written with old Gainsborough colleague Eliot Stannard and an uncredited Alma, of a romantic triangle set in the world of prize-fighting seems hardly 'Hitchcockian' in the traditional sense. It did contain, however, a crowd-pleasing montage of '18 camera dissolves in the opening fun fair sequence',[19] and a daringly authentic final bout at the Royal Albert Hall between rivals Carl Brisson (a one-time boxer) and Ian Hunter in which the latter was genuinely pugilised. 'Challenges comparison with the best that America can produce,' proclaimed the *Daily Herald*. But although the critics seemed to like it, the film wasn't, according to Hitchcock, a commercial hit. But that didn't stop the flow with, in quick succession, *The Farmer's Wife* – during the shooting of which the Hitchcocks' only child Patricia was born – *Champagne* and *The Manxman*.

Filming *Champagne* was, it seems, a particular irritation to him maybe due to the fact that it's only *raison d'être*, Hitchcock later claimed, seemed to be its fizzy title. It might also have had to do with the fact it was based on a novel by a former critic Walter Mycroft who had recently been appointed head of BIP's story department. A hunchback, he would become increasingly powerful and authoritative at Elstree, earning the nickname, 'Czar of all the Rushes'. Fed up with the project and also his leading lady Betty Balfour, Hitchcock made his feelings perfectly clear during shooting with the odd tantrum and a decision to keep the publicity stills photographer well away from the set, much to the 'front office's' displeasure. This was challenge enough for the aspiring filmmaker Michael Powell then working as a reader in the story department and determined to 'get on'. Armed with his cameras, he strode onto the troubled set. 'Hitch … was sitting in his director's chair twiddling his thumbs, He really was the fattest young man I had ever seen. He had a fresh, rosy complexion, his dark hair was sleeked back and he was correctly dressed in a suit with a watch-chain across his waistcoat. He wore a soft hat. He observed me out of the corner of his piggy eyes sunk in fat cheeks. There was not much that Hitch missed with those piggy eyes.'[20]

Powell's *chutzpah* worked as he and Hitchcock became firm friends. He also shot stills on *The Manxman* – which despite its title was mostly filmed in Somerset and North Cornwall – during which Hitchcock showed him the play script for *Blackmail* by Charles Bennett. Powell told him he thought that with work especially the addition of a big climactic chase it would make a good film. What they didn't discuss was what had just happened in Hollywood which was, of course, the arrival of sound – as in 'You ain't seen nuthin' yet', bellowed by Al Jolson in *The Jazz Singer*. *Blackmail*, the tense story of Alice (Anny Ondra) who accidentally kills a would-be rapist only to have the screws put on her by an opportunist extortionist (Donald Calthrop) began filming as a full-fledged silent until John Maxwell decided that he better yield to fashion – some still thought a passing fad – by adding dialogue in the last reel and then advertise the result as 'part talking'. Hitchcock was, however, several steps ahead of him and he knew that the film as constructed could, with more work, go the whole hog, as it were. From there 'it was a short step to getting them to allow him to re-shoot certain key scenes as a fully fledged talking picture'.[21]

Probably the most talked-about addition was the scene where early on after Alice has returned home, she is having breakfast

Hitchcock: Now, Miss Ondra, we are going to do a sound test. Isn't that what you wanted? Now come right over here.

Anny Ondra: I don't know what to say. I'm so nervous.

Hitch: Have you been a good girl?

Ondra (*laughing*): Oh, no.

Hitch: No? Have you slept with men?

Ondra: No!

Hitch: No?!

Ondra: Oh, Hitch, you make me embarrassed! (*She giggles helplessly*)

Hitch: Now come over here and stand still in your place, or it won't come out right, as the girl said to the soldier.

(*Ondra dissolves into laughter*)

Hitch: (*grinning*) Cut![22]

Sound test on *Blackmail*

with her family and all they can talk about is the local stabbing the night before. We hear the scene through her ears, as it were, with the repeated use of the word 'knife' drilling into her head as she tries to come to terms guiltily with what has transpired, a fact given an extra irony when it transpires her detective boyfriend (John Longden) is in charge of the case. Then there's Powell's uncredited chase in the British Museum towards the end of the film which actually had to be staged at the studio using what was called the Schufftan Process (after Eugen Schufftan who first developed it for Lang's *Metropolis*) where mirrors were combined with miniatures to back-project an image.

Hitchcock did, however, suddenly encounter one major problem when it came to adding dialogue. The Polish-born and Czech-raised Anny Ondra could hardly speak English so he had to employ the actress Joan Barry to 'dub' Ondra's lines live while standing at the side of the set. Unfortunately, as Paul Condon and Jim Sangster comment in *The Complete Hitchcock*, 'Barry's accent was more Royal Family than East End shop girl. As a consequence, Ondra fails to appear natural in any of her scenes containing dialogue. She's trying to throw off the shackles of the silent screen, and many of her mannerisms come across as severely overplayed. However, her jerky movements immediately following the murder are quite chilling, where she emerges from the bed still holding the knife and looking off into the distance blankly.'[23] But even that resulting awkwardness didn't detract too much from the sheer brio of Hitchcock's overall style which captivated critics and audiences alike (who also lapped up his first properly recognisable cameo role, as a London Underground passenger being pestered by a small boy). But as with *The Lodger*, he had once again, for commercial reasons, to substitute a much more ambiguous fate for Alice with an overtly happy ending:

'the girl couldn't be left to face her fate. And that shows you how films suffer from their own power of appealing to millions. They could often be subtler than they are, but their own popularity won't let them.'[24] There was, though, nothing remotely subtle about the film's marketing, with posters ballyhooing: 'The first full length all talkie film made in Great Britain. SEE & HEAR it – our mother tongue as it should be – spoken! 100% talkie, 100% entertainment. Hold everything till you've heard this one!'

With his gathering fame as well as, unusually for a director, a public profile thanks to his cameo, an increasingly healthy bank balance, a loving, talented wife (who apart from a sabbatical for pregnancy worked creatively beside him), and a new daughter, life was good for Hitchcock. He was, for example, able to fork out on a country cottage, called 'Winter's Grace', with a large garden and private strip of woodland in the village of Shamley Green, south of London between Guildford and Cranleigh. The Cromwell Road flat and Elstree remained, however, his principal commute as he then worked on a series of films which, for a while at least, only rarely seemed to add up to what he himself would have designated 'a Hitchcock movie'. He was, for example, one of four directors on *Elstree Calling*, a portmanteau effort comprising vaudeville sketches starring some of the comedy talents of the day like Tommy Handley and Gordon Harker. *Juno and The Paycock*, based on Sean O'Casey's famous play set around the Troubles at the turn of the 1920s, remained resolutely theatrical. Another successful play, by John Galsworthy, was the basis for *The Skin Game*, a story of feuding families, which had previously been filmed as a silent in 1920, also continued to be stage bound. *Rich and Strange*, an intriguing idea about kicking over the traces, had just the odd chilling moment such as a shipwreck, while *Number Seventeen*, apart from a rather breezily tense climax involving a runaway train, is often regarded as one of the director's weakest films. As for *Waltzes from Vienna*, about the Strauss Family, the title almost speaks for itself and derided by Hitchcock as 'a musical without music, made very cheaply. It had no relation to my usual work'.[25]

Between *Juno* and *The Skin Game* was, however, the more promisingly – indeed, unequivocally – titled *Murder!*, one of Hitchcock's rare whodunits which gave him more scope for the kind of technique and innovation which was becoming his trademark. Herbert Marshall, in his first talkie, plays a juror who, convinced that an actress (Norah Baring) has been wrongly convicted of murder and sentenced to death, does his own sleuthing to try and establish her innocence. There is, for example, a fascinating and novel stream-of-consciousness monologue (denoting Marshall's inner thoughts), a clever use of 'radio' music while Marshall is shaving (a 30-piece orchestra actually had to play live behind the bathroom set) and, rather less successfully, some attempt at improvised dialogue. The production was further complicated by the fact Hitchcock had also agreed to shoot simultaneously a German version (with Alfred Abel in Marshall's role) of, at his urging – wrongly, he'd admit – the same script: 'I realised I had no ear for the German language. Many touches that were quite funny in the English version were not at all amusing in the German one, as, for instance, the ironic asides on the loss of dignity or on snobbishness. The German actor was ill at ease and I came to realise I simply didn't know enough about the German idiom.'[26]

Although you could hardly call it Hitchcock's 'stock company', various names tended to recur front and back of camera during this period including actors like John Longden, Donald Calthrop, Phyllis Konstam and Edmund Gwenn. Even more regular were crew members such as assistant director Frank Mills and, most prolifically, lighting cameraman Jack Cox, who, starting with *The Ring*, photographed no fewer than 11 of Hitchcock's films in the late 1920s and early 1930s before coming back into the fold at the end of the decade with *The Lady Vanishes*. Starting with *Murder!* – 'the best of them without a doubt'[27] – Bryan Langley worked as Cox's assistant on four of the films and even earned a joint credit – 'in smaller type, mind you'[28] – on *Number Seventeen* for his contribution. 'Hitchcock once asked me if I wanted to be a cameraman and when I said "yes" he said I should go and study half a dozen of the world's best paintings and memorise the lighting techniques of the canvases and how, for instance, artists dealt with black cats in black cellars. He was a master of everything and, in particular, he had the ability to draw what he wanted to see on screen and do the perspective like a lens. For example, with a one-inch lens you get a wide background behind the actors, and as the angle narrows you get a smaller background. He was literally able to draw a set-up and show the amount of background, which could be seen with each individual lens.'[29]

Hitchcock was also contracted to film *Lord Camber's Ladies*, scripted by the playwright Benn Levy, who'd provided much of the dialogue for *Blackmail*. By now, he was thoroughly disillusioned with life at Elstree and so acted as producer only, giving Levy his directorial break. Although now finally free of his contract with BIP, *Waltzes From Vienna*, his first film for Gaumont-British, seemed to convince Hitchcock that his intermittently brilliant career had just reached 'its lowest ebb'.[30] However, also in the back of his still fertile mind was a project, a Bulldog Drummond story he'd developed with *Blackmail* author Charles Bennett and Edwin Greenwood, which had been given strangely short shrift by John Maxwell. Hitchcock suspected there was more to

41

Maxwell's rejection than met the eye so he had left BIP with no regrets. Then one day, Michael Balcon strode on to the set of *Waltzes From Vienna*. Balcon was by now director of production for Gainsborough and its mother company, Gaumont-British – vertically integrated like BIP with cinemas and a distribution 'arm' too – whose film-making base was its Lime Grove Studios at Shepherds Bush, recently rebuilt at a cost of £500,000. Balcon asked him about his next project and Hitchcock mentioned the Drummond yarn, which appealed to him. However, *Bulldog Drummond's Baby* was about to turn into *The Man Who Knew Too Much*, the film that 're-established my creative prestige'.[31]

Chapter 4

Mastering Suspense

Hitchcock's Technicolorful re-make in 1956 of *The Man Who Knew Too Much*, with James Stewart and Doris Day, not to mention its Oscar-winning song, 'Que Sera, Sera', is much better known than his 1934 original. But if one is looking for clues to the future, a kind of template if you like, then you need go no further than this stylishly tricksy monochrome comedy thriller which properly set Hitchcock on his way to earning the enduring tag of 'Master of Suspense'. First developed as a kidnap tale involving the child of Sapper's famous sleuth, Hitchcock and his co-writers – ultimately, no fewer than five of them including Charles Bennett and Emlyn Williams – eventually decided to drop the idea of Bulldog Drummond and concentrate instead on an 'ordinary' holidaying couple, Bob (Leslie Banks) and Jill (Edna Best), who are suddenly caught up in international events beyond their control. This includes the abduction of their little daughter Betty (15-year-old Nova Pilbeam) by a group of assassins as leverage for her parents' silence. The project re-introduced Hitchcock to his old champion, Ivor Montagu, who had been hired by Balcon to act as associate producer on future films from

Gaumont-British's new and much-prized signing. As they worked up the new script, Bennett commented, 'it was indeed pleasant to work with Hitchcock then, although he had a monstrous ego that matched his appetite'.[32]

The film opens in snowy St Moritz – where the Hitchcocks had spent their honeymoon – before moving back to congested London, a contrast that the director wanted visually and emotionally to underpin the whole production. He also had a couple of other 'musts', Hitchcock insisted on casting Peter Lorre as the main villain, despite the fact that his English was extremely sketchy at the start of shooting. The Hungarian-born Lorre who become world-famous three years earlier playing the child-killer in Fritz Lang's *M* had only recently fled Nazi Germany when he signed on to play the tiny but deadly Mr Abbott. The production also coincided with Lorre's marriage in London to the first of his three wives, undertaken during a two-hour break in shooting and with the actor still wearing the vivid make-up scar across his temple required for the role. For the film's climax, a rooftop shoot-out, Hitchcock's model was the notoriously violent 1911 Sidney Street siege during which the police, eventually joined by army reinforcements, had cornered a group of East European anarchists in the East End. Pre-production scrutiny of scripts by the film censor was commonplace and it was made very clear to Hitchcock that the idea of depicting police use of firearms was extremely undesirable. Surely the baddies could be flushed out with water hoses? In the end, Hitchcock managed to get round the problem rather ingeniously with a suitably distracting if occasionally grisly finale, which also involved crack-shot Jill Lawrence picking off one of the gang with a rifle she's snatched from one of the police officers.

The film is, however, probably best known for its superbly

Leslie Banks and Nova Pilbeam holding a daschund to give authenticity to the Alpine setting of the 1934 version of The Man Who Knew too Much

45

mounted principal set-piece – the planned assassination of an important foreign diplomat at the Albert Hall. Hitchcock's initial plan was to have Jill carrying out the killing while in a hypnotic trance. On mature reflection it was felt that even though it had been established from the film's outset that she was a marksman might require too great a suspension of disbelief to imagine she could take out the ambassador in her induced state. Instead, they came up with a sweatily effective crowd-pleaser, which, in effect, completely reversed the original idea. We learn that the killer is to strike during a clash of cymbals in the middle of a cantata (especially composed for the film by Arthur Benjamin) so Hitchcock builds up tension in the minutest detail, in particular to make sure audience attention is firmly on those cymbals and precisely at which point the clash itself is to arrive during the music – 'knowing what to expect, they wait for it to happen. This conditioning of the viewer is essential to the build-up of suspense … I've often found that a suspense situation is weakened because the action is not sufficiently clear.'[33] Knowing the location of the assassination, though not, like us, its precise timing, Jill arrives at the Albert Hall where she sees the killer Ramon (Frank Vosper) who, warning her again of Betty's dire straits, heads for a reserved box to initiate his dirty deed. With the tension now strung out to its very limit, Jill finally cracks and screams loudly just as the cymbals crash thankfully putting Ramon off his shot, thus alerting the police to his presence and accelerating the final denouement at the villains' den.

The film proved to be a huge success, but not before, extraordinarily, the kind of serious 'front office' doubts which had also attended Hitchcock's earlier, edgier films. In fact, C M Woolf, head of Gaumont-British's distribution department, seemingly held out no hope of any commercial prospects whatsoever for a film, which he regarded as 'utter nonsense'.[34] Wiser counsel and, notably once again, the good sense of Ivor Montagu prevailed and despite a brief premiere run on the bottom half of a double-feature, the cream, accompanied by some lavishly good reviews, quickly rose to the top. Questioned 30 years later by François Truffaut, Hitchcock was asked to draw comparisons between the two versions of the film. He concluded, perhaps rather too self-deprecatingly, 'Let's say that the first version is the work of a talented amateur and the second was made by a professional.'[35]

At first, Woolf's reservations were enough to put some serious frighteners under Hitchcock who was already thinking ahead to his next project. 'Let's not even go ahead with *The 39 Steps*, because they'll never finance it. There's nothing I can do.'[36] Hitchcock declared miserably in a phone call to his collaborator, Charles Bennett. A contemporary of H C 'Sapper' McNeile, Buchan's much better crafted ripping yarns of snobbery-with-violence had long appealed to Hitchcock who once entertained plans of making *Greenmantle*. Having eschewed Sapper's Bulldog Drummond for *The Man Who Knew Too Much*, a decidedly Buchan-esque adventure, it didn't seem too much of a stretch to imagine why he settled on the author's most popular gentleman hero, Richard Hannay, for his next film, an adaptation of Buchan's eve-of-the-Great War novel, probably the author's most popular work. If not precisely Buchan's story in terms of real menace – and not even a pair of subsequent remakes by others (in 1959 and 1978) managed it either – Hitchcock's is easily the closest to the spirit of the original as well as being quite daringly innovative in its own right and, despite its great age, still deliciously timeless. 'What I find appealing in Buchan's work is his understatement of highly dramatic ideas,'[37] said Hitchcock and in that aspect his fidelity is admirable. Above all, the film, just 81 minutes long, has that breathless quality that perfectly matches its short sharp innocent-on-the-run scenario in yet another modification of the kind of plotline which was destined to become a Hitchcock staple.

The story, which begins with Hannay (Robert Donat) becoming unwittingly involved in murder and the theft of state secrets, is, according to Hitchcock, deliberately episodic – a series of short, ever more spectacular set-pieces that could almost be self-contained little films in their own right. A typical example is an early scene – a complete invention of the scenarists – when the fleeing Hannay is holed up in a remote corner of Scotland with a gruff crofter (John Laurie) and his lonely young wife (Peggy Ashcroft). The sexual tension during this brief *ménage à trois* is palpable. Like with so many of Hitchcock's more obviously famous cinema moments, the wicked sense of unease is mostly unspoken, as if he'd always prefer to trust the visual rather than the verbal for maximum audience effect. The sequence, Hitchcock has said, was inspired by an altogether more overtly risqué story but, as would happen more and more frequently in the director's work, it's what you *don't* see – notable the first killing in *Psycho* – that often works best.

There's another, albeit lighter-hearted, kind of sexual *frisson* in the scenes between our hero and the lovely Pamela (Madeleine Carroll), who suddenly finds herself trapped in Hannay's unfolding nightmare. Having first met her briefly when she gives very short shrift to Hannay during his flight north by train, we now rediscover her in the company of the police in order to formally identify him. Except that they are not the Law at all but actually enemy agents from whom Hannay, now handcuffed to the hapless Pamela, makes yet another escape. Together, she still very reluctantly, they eventually check in at a pub for the night where there is – surprise, surprise – only a double-bedded room available. Just back from Hollywood and in a part that was first offered to Jane Baxter, Carroll, generally regarded as the first official Hitchcock blonde, kick-started the tradition of being funny, feisty and often subjected to indignities on and off set. As well as some manhandling on the studio's Scottish Marshes set – all the authentic Highland scenes were filmed with doubles – she allegedly also got an unusual acting lesson from the director. 'When Hitchcock was dissatisfied with a shot in which she was required to react in horror to the appearance of a pair of sinister pursuers, [he] provoked a more extravagant reaction by whipping his penis from his trousers.'[38] Another important blonde also arrived in Hitchcock's life as *The 39 Steps* was about to begin filming. This was 24-year-old Joan Harrison, a newspaper editor's daughter born not far from her new boss's country home in Shamley Green, who, after starting out as his secretary, quickly moved up to assistant then screenwriter and finally producer of Hitchcock's television series in the 1950s. For nearly 30 years she would be the third most important woman in his life after Alma and daughter Pat.

But how to top the Albert Hall scene from his last film? Why, at the London Palladium, of course. Instead of a classical concert and clashing cymbals, we are, this time round, enjoying a touch of the vaudevilles in the company of Mr Memory (Wylie Watson) whose extraordinary powers of recall are first unveiled briefly in a music hall sequence near the beginning of the film. Its climax take place at the Palladium when Hannay realises that there is some kind of crucial link between the traitors, led by the Professor (Godfrey Tearle) with a missing finger, and poor, doomed Mr Memory, a character derived from Hitchcock's own memory of an act called Mr Datas. Hitchcock's splendid twist is

Although they didn't finally work together until 1944, screenwriter Angus MacPhail is said actually to have coined the expression 'MacGuffin' which has become an integral part of the Hitchcock filmmaking lexicon. It's a device, which though not necessarily integral to the plot, helps to drive the story forward. According to Hitchcock, there were two men on a train and one asks the other: 'What's that package up on baggage rack?' The other answers, 'That's a MacGuffin.' 'What's a MacGuffin?' the first man asks. 'Well, it's an apparatus for trapping lions in the Scottish Highlands,' the other replies. 'But there are no lions in the Scottish Highlands,' says the first man. 'Well then. That's no MacGuffin!'

that his version of the character 'is doomed by a sense of duty. Mr Memory knows what the thirty-nine steps are and when he is asked the question [by Hannay in the hearing of the police] he is *compelled* to give the answer'.[39] Incidentally, for the purposes of the film, the 'Thirty Nine Steps' is the name of a spy organisation as opposed to the crucial Kent coast location in Buchan's book. Were these 'Thirty Nine Steps' the first example of the notorious 'MacGuffin' – 'the pretext for the plot', as Truffaut defined it – which would become as regular a feature of Hitchcock's films as his cameo appearances? Actually no, said Hitchcock. In the case of *The 39 Steps*, the 'MacGuffin' – a sort of elaboration on a 'red herring' – was the state secret being sought by the spies and their plan to smuggle it out of the country via Mr Memory's brain.

Not that these kind of arcane details would particularly exercise the audiences who flocked to the film, Hitchcock's most perfectly realised to date, in Britain and in the States too where it was also rapturously received. Indeed it would be rather nice to speculate whether one of Hannay's best lines, 'There are twenty million women in this island and I get to be chained to you', made an early impression on some young Hollywood screenwriters long before they penned *Casablanca*. This didn't, however, mean a complete absence of the usual doubts in some quarters, which traditionally greeted the completion of a Hitchcock film. C M Woolf, who clearly believed the company's hottest property to be far too clever for his good would, if Michael Balcon hadn't swiftly intervened, have happily terminated Hitchcock's contract. His next project was an adaptation of a pair of Somerset Maugham spy stories, 'The Traitor' and 'The Hairless Mexican', in the author's 'Ashenden' series (about a gentleman novelist-secret agent), and of a play by George Campbell Dixon, based on them. *Secret Agent* is Hitchcock's first 'international' thriller

The original 'Hitchcock Blonde',
Madeleine Carroll starred with
John Gielgud in Secret Agent.
It was one of his earliest screen
roles for British Gaumont in
1936

with the action talking place principally in Switzerland during
the First World War where we follow Ashenden's halting attempt
to terminate an enemy agent. Many of the usual ingredients are
here, including a spectacular train crash and the man-who-isn't
what-he-first-seems (Hollywood import Robert Young) as well as
familiar faces like Madeleine Carroll and Peter Lorre.

But despite its ambitious wider canvas, perhaps out of all of
Hitchcock's more traditional canon, *Secret Agent* now looks the
most dated, probably due in no small part to the stilted performance of John Gielgud as Ashenden. Already a giant of the
London stage, he was appearing in his own production of *Romeo
and Juliet* when the theatre-loving Hitchcock cast him in his
new film. With barely a handful of film roles to his credit up till
then, Gielgud had the additional burden of having to combine
filming by day with Shakespeare by night because he and Laurence Olivier were alternating the roles of Romeo and Mercutio.
'Of course, I was paid more money than in the theatre, but I had
the feeling that no one thought I was sufficiently good-looking to
be successful … I did not have much confidence in my talent as
a film actor and I thought when I saw the film that I was rather
poor,'[40] Gielgud later wrote in his memoirs. Also, according to
Gielgud, Hitchcock made him 'feel like a jelly and … nearly sick
with nervousness',[41] as the director, pointing out that his stage
experience now counted for nothing, strove to 'make him rub
out everything and start blank'.[42] As far as the admiring Hitchcock was concerned – and the comments have to weighed care-
fully as they were probably part of a contemporaneous publicity
push – 'Gielgud's performance in the picture is remarkable',[43]
and that the actor switched from stage to screen 'with complete
conviction'.[44]

With his next two films, *Sabotage* and *Young and Innocent*,

Hitchcock was back on much firmer, as well as native, ground. However, *Sabotage* (derived, ironically in view of his previous project, from Joseph Conrad's novel, *The Secret Agent*) and *Young and Innocent*, a sort of youthful re-working of *The 39 Steps*, are like chalk and cheese – the first, dark and claustrophobic, the second, distinctly light and frothy. In *Sabotage*, Verloc (sinister, beetle-browed Oscar Homolka) runs a local cinema as a cover for his work as a saboteur for some unnamed foreign power. Neither his wife (Sylvia Sydney) nor her little brother Stevie know what he's up to but both, in the case of one, fatally, become embroiled in his orders to unleash hell on London in the form of a time bomb to be placed in Piccadilly Circus tube station. Hitchcock's main set-pieces are very cunningly wrought. When Verloc is unable to carrying out the bombing he 'recruits' the unwitting Stevie in his stead. As if it isn't bad enough we know that a device is about to explode in a public place, the innocent agent of that planned destruction is then a mere child who dies in the process – something which Hitchcock later admitted was actually 'a grave error' of judgement.[45] Naturally there's retribution for Verloc in another extraordinary scene when almost entirely in half-shot or close-up, Sylvia Sydney, in a daze following the tragic death of Stevie, stabs her husband to death at the dinner table. Hitchcock said he wanted 'to make the murder inevitable without any blame attaching to the woman. I wanted to preserve sympathy for her, so that it was essential that she fought against something stronger than herself'.[46] The implication is that the resulting death appears suitably ambiguous, even perhaps the suggestion that the guilt-ridden Verloc had, as it were, fallen on a handy sword.

Young and Innocent, from Josephine Tey's novel *A Shilling for Candles*, with Nova Pilbeam returning to the Hitchcock fold at the grand old age of 18, is essentially forgettable. That is, apart from one virtuoso piece of cinema, which suggested a very close collaboration between the director and cinematographer (later director) Bernard Knowles, who shot five of his British films including *The 39 Steps*, *Secret Agent* and *Sabotage*. Pilbeam, as the daughter of the local police chief and in love with a chap (Derrick de Marney) wrongfully accused of murder, is on the trail of the real culprit whom we know has a compulsive twitch. She and her sidekick, an old tramp (Edward Rigby), think they have bearded him during a tea dance in the ballroom of the Grand Hotel. In one 70-second shot, the camera starts to make its way across and high above the room working slowly down towards the music and the orchestra of players in blackface. It heads on for the drummer in the back row frantically flailing away, finally moving in tight so that it actually frames his twitching eyes.

Between *Sabotage* and *Young and Innocent*, there was a serious industry crisis brewing. By the beginning of 1937 it became clear that even with government incentives in the form of indigenous filmmaking known as 'Quota Quickies', British films simply didn't have enough international – and in particular, American – clout to guarantee the success of UK studios. It was still, however, a shock when Hitchcock's backers, Gaumont-British, announced it was going to close down its principal studio at Shepherd's Bush. Michael Balcon – who two years later would begin his long stewardship of Ealing Films – and Ivor Montagu were fired while Hitchcock's contract was taken over by Gainsborough. The most immediate problem for Hitchcock was that in the midst of shooting *Young and Innocent*, he suddenly had to switch studios, from Lime Grove to Pinewood which was then in its first flush of activity before later becoming Britain's premier film factory. Hitchcock, now at the height of his British fame, enjoyed an enviable lifestyle and growing international reputation while also indulging in expensive holidays and acquiring some decent art. It was surely just a matter of time before Hitchcock, who as a teenager knew New York by heart from just studying maps, would get that inevitable Hollywood offer.

Chapter 5

Hooray for Hollywood

In a memo dated 23 August 1937 to his New York Story Editor, Katharine 'Kay' Brown, American producer David O Selznick wrote: 'I AM DEFINITELY INTERESTED IN HITCHCOCK AS A DIREC-TOR AND THINK IT MIGHT BE WISE FOR YOU TO MEET AND CHAT WITH HIM. IN PARTICULAR I WOULD LIKE TO GET A CLEAR PICTURE AS TO WHO, IF ANYONE, IS REPRESENTING HIM AND WHAT HE HAS IN MIND IN THE WAY OF A SALARY ...'.[47] Three months later, Hitch-cock, by now fully aware of Selznick's 'feelers' and having earlier that same year excitedly made his first ever visit with Alma and Pat to the States, started shooting *The Lady Vanishes* at Islington Studios. With, in the back of his mind, an old story about the bizarre and inexplicable disappearance of a woman at the 1889 Paris Exhibition, Hitchcock worked with the writing team of Frank Launder and Sidney Gilliat for a project – an adaptation of Ethel Lina White's novel *The Wheel Spins* – first announced to the press as *Lost Lady*. In fact, a year before Hitchcock became involved there had been an attempt to produce it but it had been shelved after a film unit, sent to Yugoslavia for some location shooting, had encountered a little local difficulty. The government, 'fearful of upsetting Adolf Hitler, had taken exception to one scene [in the script] in which a shot of goose-stepping soldiers dissolved into another of waddling geese.'[48] Hitchcock loved Launder and Gilliat's script which despite, or perhaps because of, his inevitable additions, subtractions and amendments – notably a new shoot-'em-up ending – still remains among the wittiest of all his films. For their part, Launder and Gilliat never fully appreciated the fact that Hitchcock would, for the first time put his name 'above the title'. Interestingly, they and another pair, Michael Powell and Emeric Pressburger, would in their own time and in their own fashion, establish their own unique styles of British film-making following Hitchcock's exit to Hollywood.

At £80,000, modestly budgeted even by his previous standards, *The Lady Vanishes*, with its fast-paced trans-European tale of international intrigue, was filmed principally on just one, cramped, 90-foot set complete with the mock-up of a railway carriage. Back projection and some less than convincing miniatures provided a bigger canvas. For 21-year-old second assistant director Roy Ward Baker, it was like a crash course in filmmaking: 'To start with Hitchcock's methodical approach. He boasted that he always had the film fully worked out in his mind's eye before he started shooting … and as we came to each set, one of my duties was to obtain from the art department a number of copies of a small-scale outline plan of the set. I put them in Hitchcock's office each day before lunch … after lunch each day I collected the plans from the office. Hitch had drawn each set-up on them as he intended to shoot it the following day, in some cases specifying the lens … with such full and accurate information, you couldn't fail and he never double-crossed you by changing his mind.'[49] Such a degree of pre-planning didn't, of course, allow for the odd spanner. For example, one of the

Michael Redgrave gets to grips with a troublesome nun in The Lady Vanishes. *Dame May Whitty and Margaret Lockwood on the left*

actresses, Linden Travers, decided that a planned two-shot of her in profile with Paul Lukas, as the outwardly charming-but-ultimately shifty surgeon Dr Hartz, didn't favour her best 'side'. So she persuaded the lighting cameraman Jack Cox, back on Hitchcock duty for the 11th and final time, to let her change places with Lukas. With the set-up and lighting complete, Hitchcock was called back to the set and in an instant knew there was something radically different from his blueprint. He then proceeded to make a meal of his obviously feigned bafflement to everyone's increasing discomfort until Travers knew the game was up and sloped back into her original window seat. Recalled Ward Baker: 'Maybe Paul Lukas's left profile was the better. Maybe it was a matter of principle, More likely the man was indulging himself at the poor girl's expense. I am sure Hitchcock hated actors.'[50]

The film's two main stars were Margaret Lockwood, who already had more than a dozen film roles under her belt at 21, and Michael Redgrave, eight years her senior and a stage veteran, who'd previously only enjoyed a spit-and-cough in *Secret Agent*. His rather actory concern at the lack of preparation for a particular scene was given very short shrift by Hitchcock. 'In the theatre, we'd have three weeks to rehearse this,' Redgrave complained to the director. 'I'm sorry,' came the terse reply, 'in this medium we have three minutes.'[51] But that was mild compared with his treatment of venerable seventysomething Dame May Whitty, playing governess-cum-spy Miss Froy, the lady who vanishes. In the middle of her first scene, Hitchcock yelled at her, 'Stop! That's terrible. Aren't you ashamed of yourself?'[52] This assault seems to have been part of a concerted ploy to assert his authority, judging by a comment he reportedly made later to producer Edward Black: 'Break 'em down at the start – it's much the better way'.[53] Incidentally, during the casting process for Miss Froy, one of the actresses up for the role was Marjorie Fielding, who just happened to be an old family friend of David Harcourt, a young camera assistant on the film. He recalled her audition: 'She was very nervous and I did what I could to steady her. Then, before her test, Hitch came up to me and whispered, "Don't put any film in the camera." That was like a stab wound to me. I felt terrible. But what could I do; I was just the assistant. After Hitch called "Cut", he told her, "Thank you very much, we'll let you

know." Naturally she came up to me and asked how I thought it had all gone. "Fine," I said, stuttering. Now, of course, I was acting.'

A doubtless chastened Whitty – who could have hardly imagined that nearly 70 years later scenes of her from the film would be morphed into a contemporary commercial for Virgin Trains – she proves to be one of many highlights of the film which also contains a wonderful running joke – or is it? – about 'England in crisis'. This seems to refer to the very serious business of Europe perched on the edge of another world war as a train-load of disparate characters hurtle through Nazi-occupied lands. For two of them, Charters and Caldicott (Basil Radford and Naunton Wayne, in the first of what would become a comic double-act), it's a different kind of crisis altogether. England are right up against it in the latest cricket test match and they are rushing home to try and lend their support in the team's time of need. A 'MacGuffin' of the highest order.

One suspects this deliciously parochial in-joke was lost on Selznick who, following up his interest in Hitchcock the previous summer, sent a memo to him in January 1938 saying: 'SAW "LADY VANISHES" LAST NIGHT AND I LOVE YOU …'[54] before filling him in with the latest news about a project that the producer, who'd yet to finalise the film rights on a book which was still three months away from publication, was hoping might prove to be Hitchcock's Hollywood debut – Daphne du Maurier's *Rebecca*. Hitchcock had known the author ever since working with her father Gerald on *Lord Camber's Ladies* in 1932, and once had the opportunity to buy the rights himself to the book, her fifth. By this time, he was being seriously wooed by America and was even offered the chance by RKO to direct *The Saint in New York*, which he somehow resisted. Selznick was, in fact, juggling two

David O Selznick (1902–65), born in Pittsburgh, began working in the film industry as a publicist and story analyst for his father Lewis Selznick. He then worked for MGM, Paramount and RKO in various production capacities before forming his own company, Selznick International Pictures in 1936 which would, by 1940, with films like *Gone with the Wind*, *Rebecca* and *Intermezzo* be the top money-making film company in Hollywood. Increasing tax problems, however, eventually brought his empire crashing down. His second wife was the actress Jennifer Jones.

David O Selznick and Hitchcock in discussion on the set of Rebecca

huge projects at the time – *Rebecca* and, of course, *Gone With the Wind*. Despite some resistance from his board chairman, Jock Whitney, who'd suddenly cooled on Hitchcock after finally catching up with *Young and Innocent*, Selznick was like a dogged fisherman determined to land a big catch. When negotiations for *Rebecca* began to prove tricky, Selznick then dangled another carrot, a film about the *Titanic* disaster. Still keeping his options open, Hitchcock decided that all this American interest was excuse enough for him to make his first, strangely belated, foray to the film capital. Which he did in a way, by air to New York then transcontinental rail to Los Angeles, that would certainly have appealed to the boy who loved trains and timetables.

On his own patch, Selznick's lure finally proved irresistible and Hitchcock was all but signed and sealed for what was first mooted as a seven-year, four-film deal at $40,000 per film. When the actual deal was announced on 2 July in Hollywood, the conditions were much less long-term but significantly more lucrative with Hitchcock inked in at $50,000 for just the one film. This was huge money by the director's previous standards, indeed a veritable fortune compared with what he was earning when, in the mid 1920s as still jack-of-all-trades on *The Passionate Adventure*, Hitchcock first met, and became friendly with, Selznick's older brother Myron, whose agency now represented him. *The Titanic* quickly proved to be stillborn but not before Hitchcock who, it seems, never seriously entertained the idea of tackling such a subject, joked somewhat mean-spiritedly to an enquiring reporter, 'Oh, yes, I've had experience with icebergs. Don't forget, I directed Madeleine Carroll.'[55] *Rebecca* was now firmly set as his US debut which meant he had time on his hands before he needed to re-locate to the States for a planned start of shooting towards the end of 1939.

With his international stock never higher following the award of Best Film from the New York Film Critics for *The Lady Vanishes*, Hitchcock suddenly found himself, against his better judgement, signing up for *Jamaica Inn*, based on Daphne du Maurier's fourth novel, a fruity period Cornish smuggling tale. He hated the first draft of the script by playwright Clemence Dane so much that he sought every conceivable way of backing out of the assignment. It was only the persistence of the star Charles Laughton, who was also co-producer, a re-write by Sidney Gilliat and the promise of some additional dialogue by J B Priestley that kept Hitchcock reluctantly in the game but, as he'd later comment, it was 'an absurd thing to undertake'.[56] He also noted, revealingly, 'It isn't possible to direct a Charles Laughton film, the best you can hope is to act as referee,' adding more in sorrow than in anger, '[Charles] never became a craft professional.'[57] Another cross to bear was Laughton's German refugee co-producer Erich Pommer, an old sparring partner from Neubabelsberg days on *The Blackguard*. Yet although *Jamaica Inn* is, along with the likes of *Waltzes from Vienna*, about as far from what the director himself would describe as 'a Hitchcock picture' as you can get, the end result is oddly endearing. There's so much ripe ham on display – especially when Laughton, as the duplicitous squire, and younger co-star Robert Newton are in full flow – it's like indulging in an extremely tasty pig roast.

Throughout the entire shooting schedule of *Jamaica Inn* towards the back end of 1938, Hitchcock was also becoming increasingly pre-occupied with *Rebecca*, whose film rights now firmly resided with Selznick. As he battled with Laughton and Pommer at Elstree Studios, he was also subjected to a barrage of transatlantic memos from the producer ranging from the right screenwriter to whether there should be first-person narration.

Robert Newton, Charles Laughton, Leslie Banks and Maureen O'Hara in **Jamaica Inn** – *a piece of ripe ham*

When Selznick suggested the likes of Ben Hecht, Sidney Howard and Clemence Dane, Hitchcock swiftly countered with Lillian Hellman and Sidney Gilliat while making his negative feelings about Dane especially clear. For the time being he and his assistant Joan Harrison worked away on the first treatment of the script and continued to do so after they, together with Alma and 10-year-old Pat boarded the *Queen Mary* at Southampton on 1 March 1939 for the voyage to America. Also in the Hitchcock entourage were a cook, maid and 'two small dogs – the dark spaniel, Edward IX (so named following the abdication of the previous king), and the white Sealyham, Mr Jenkins'.[58] With the Cromwell Road flat leased out, the regular household was on the move. After a few days on the East Coast – during which time Hitchcock found time to lecture on suspense to the Yale Drama School – and a brief family holiday in Florida, the entourage finally arrived in Los Angeles. There, they took up residence at a luxuriously-appointed three-bedroom apartment on Wilshire Boulevard, conveniently situated within easy driving distance – and memo bombardment range – of the Selznick studio in Culver City.

Selznick himself was immersed in *Gone With the Wind*, now nearly four months into shooting but that didn't stop him from regularly putting his oar in on his other pet project. Hitchcock, happily adapting to his new lotus life in the Californian sun, must have been deeply stung by the furious memo which arrived on 12 June in which Selznick declared he was 'shocked and disappointed beyond words' by the treatment firmly adding, in case there was any demur, 'we bought *Rebecca* and we intend to make *Rebecca*'.[59] For Selznick, fidelity to the original was paramount as he obliquely criticised Hitchcock for making changes for what he regarded simply as change's sake. In a fascinating aside which echoes down to this day, he noted, 'I have never been able to understand why motion-picture people insist upon throwing away something of proven appeal to substitute things of their own creation. It is a form of ego which has very properly drawn upon Hollywood the wrath of the world for many years …'[60] In less of a memo, more a monograph, Selznick was particularly exercised by 'cheap' attempts at humour which included a boat scene in which the audience is first introduced to the brooding Maxim de

Winter when his cigar-smoking causes seasickness among fellow passengers. One suspects that this kind of black comedy had especially appealed to Hitchcock and probably, wrongly, clouds his less-than-fond recollection of the film when he discussed it eventually with Truffaut – 'Well, it's not a Hitchcock picture; it's a novelette, really. The story is old-fashioned; there was a whole school of feminine literature at the period, and though I'm not against it, the fact is that the story is lacking in humour.'[61]

The offending material, which had been given an extra polish by Scots-born Philip MacDonald, the experienced ex-pat screen-writer and novelist, was just one of the many problems now facing Hitchcock in the countdown to the scheduled start of shooting on 8 September. Ronald Colman, William Powell and even David Niven were all in the frame at one time or another for Maxim before the role went to Laurence Olivier, hot on the heels of his success as Heathcliff in *Wuthering Heights*. Not unnaturally, the actor hoped that the anonymous heroine of du Maurier's novel, who gets caught up in the gothic world of de Winter and his sinister Manderley home, might be played by his bride-to-be, Vivien Leigh, who was otherwise currently occupied on Civil War film business. She did, however, find time to screen test unsuccessfully along with a directory full of other actresses including Hitchcock 'vet' Nova Pilbeam and 16-year-old Anne Baxter. With three weeks to go, Joan Fontaine, born in Tokyo to British parents and long Selznick's own preferred choice, signed on. In the final countdown to filming, with a script now bearing the additional credits of another British writer, Michael Hogan, and the distinguished American playwright, Robert E Sherwood, Selznick wrote (to his wife Irene) of Hitchcock, 'He's not a bad guy, shorn of affectations, although not exactly a man to go camping with.'[62]

No sooner was Selznick International Studios rid of one, recreated war, then the real thing suddenly exploded in the background just five days before cameras began turning on *Rebecca* with the outbreak of the Second World War in Europe. Along with his principally expatriate, so-called 'Hollywood Raj', cast – including Nigel Bruce, Gladys Cooper, C Aubrey Smith and Adelaide-born Judith Anderson, playing Fontaine's malign nemesis, Mrs Danvers – Hitchcock's thoughts quickly turned to rather more

Joan Fontaine greets her co-stars Gladys Cooper and Nigel Bruce on the set of Rebecca. *The all-English cast of the film marked one of the high-water marks of the 'Raj' in Hollywood*

weighty matters than his $950,000-budgeted melodrama. His mother back home happily re-assured him that it was still strictly a 'phoney war' and that there was no immediate likelihood of bombs raining on London. And no, she told him, she had no desire, as he was now mooting, to move to the States. Hitchcock's cosy, albeit hard-working, exile meant he wasn't immune from criticism, notably by his old friend, Michael Balcon, who later, passionately if rather intemperately, accused him of deserting the old country in its hour of need. Adding some fuel to this potential blaze was the fact that Hitchcock's Hollywood debut turned out to be so … well, British. As Hitchcock himself would later comment: 'It's a completely British picture: the story, the actors and the director were all English. I've sometimes wondered what that picture would have been like had it been made in England with the same cast. I'm not sure I would have handled it in the same way.'[63] As for the heinous accusation of desertion Hitchcock could retort that like Alexander Korda, who was also producing films Stateside, 'he was continuing filmmaking in America at the express request of the British Government.'[64]

However 'British' *Rebecca* might have been with in its actual ingredients, the resulting feast is Hollywood at its most elegant and edible. Selznick's immense influence – apparent via his voluminous memos throughout production and well into the cutting room – is conspicuous in everything from individual performances, especially Fontaine's, to even minor pieces of editing. He even chided Hitchcock for letting the script girl read off-scene lines rather than the principal involved in two-shot scenes. Does this suggest that Hitchcock was simply a cipher for Selznick? Despite the director's own reservations about the film, there are still some obvious personal touches – and not just the traditional cameo in which he can be spotted waiting in line at a telephone

kiosk. The obsessive Mrs Danvers, as played by Judith Ander-son under Hitchcock's careful guidance, is like something out of some terrifying fairy-tale, a marvellous screen creation who brings the audience up with a jolt almost every time she appears, still and sinister, on screen. He'd also, thankfully, got his own way with the film's final shot. Selznick was determined that as Manderley blazed, a curl of smoke should somehow form an 'R' in the sky above the crumbling mansion. Instead, Hitchcock

Judith Anderson's role as Mrs Danvers gave Rebecca *one of the most sinister female figures in all of Hitchcock's films. She is seen here menacing Joan Fontaine who played the second Mrs de Winter*

quickly 'busked' a scene where the flames reduce the 'R' on a pillowcase to ashes as the ghost of Rebecca (Max's first wife) is finally exorcised.

The film was a huge hit both critically and commercially and the deserving Anderson just one of its 11 nominees for Academy Awards in 1940. In the end it actually won only two – for Best Picture and Best Cinematography (George Barnes). Hitchcock, in the first of five unsuccessful nominations for Best Director over the next 20 years, was pipped on this occasion by John Ford (*Grapes of Wrath*). Selznick, a year after he'd picked up the same award for *Gone With the Wind*, was, of course, the only recipient name on the statuette when he went up to receive it at Los Angeles's Biltmore Hotel. The occasion was especially notable as being the first Oscar ceremony at which the winners were kept secret until the actual hand-over and at which the US President played a part in the proceedings. Via a six-minute live radio feed from the White House, Franklin D Roosevelt, with his country still more than nine months away from war, addressed the 1,500 guests with some appropriately stirring words on national defence and solidarity.

By the time they actually attended the 13th Awards banquet, presided over by Bob Hope, the Hitchcocks were not only well ensconced in their first house – by Hollywood-standards a surprisingly modest home on Saint Cloud Road, Bel-Air – but he'd already completed another two and half films, including his first for the British 'war effort'.

At home in Hollywood, Hitchcock leans on the balcony of the apartment in the Wilshire Palms in Los Angeles

Chapter 6

At War

The Battle of Britain had been raging for a little over six weeks when, from London, Michael Balcon, who had just started running Ealing Studios, launched his own attack on Hitchcock in the *Sunday Dispatch*. Citing all 'who prefer to remain in Hollywood instead of returning home to aid their country's war efforts', he singled out his protégé – who'd celebrated his 41st birthday two weeks earlier – for withering mention. 'I had a plump young junior technician in my studios, whom I promoted from department to department,' growled Balcon, 'Today he is one of our most famous directors and he is in Hollywood while we who are left behind short-handed are trying to harness the films to our great national effort.'

Ironically, Balcon's onslaught was published only two days before the New York premiere of Hitchcock's second film, *Foreign Correspondent*, which arguably did more effective anti-Nazi flag-waving than anything he might have managed had he been merely assisting the Allied propaganda effort back in his homeland. At the end of 1939, America, still nearly two years away from joining the war, was surely ready for an urgent reminder of the totali-

tarian horrors occurring just a continent away and where/who better, Hitchcock must have reasoned, than Hollywood/himself to effect this. On the day of the premiere, Hitchcock bit back at Balcon in the columns of the *New York World-Telegram*, describing him 'as a permanent Donald Duck. We have all placed ourselves at the disposal of our government … The manner of which I am helping my country is not Mr Balcon's business and has

Hitchcock together with Alma and Patricia take their dogs, Edward IX and Mr Jenkins, out for a walk near their apartment in Hollywood

nothing to do with patriotic ideals. Mr Balcon apparently hates Hollywood. I can only put his remarks down as personal jealousy. How else could he be so unintelligent?'

A fortnight after this sadly bitter exchange of views, the so-called German Blitz on London began in earnest. Brother William, whose fish shop was bombed out in the south of the capital, went to live at Shamley Green where he joined his doughty mother who still refused all entreaties from her second son to join him and the family in California. Not even a short visit home by him to check personally on her welfare could persuade the 77-year-old matriarch. Alma, who'd bring her own mother and sister to the States without any demur, was, it seems, particularly hurt by Balcon's words and she soon resolved to take out American citizenship, a long process (not completed until 1950) which began with acquiring naturalisation papers.

After *Rebecca* – which had been in production throughout the first months of the war – Hitchcock was still under contract to Selznick but without a suitable project to undertake while the producer stepped back for a while from active filmmaking. He was, effectively, a free agent and available for 'loan' to any other producer who could come up with properly tasty assignment especially if it meant that he could also do a little something for the old country. *Personal History*, the memoirs of the distinguished foreign correspondent Vincent Sheean, had been published in 1936 and purchased for $10,000 by Walter Wanger who tried without success to set up a film version over the next two years. Apparently the banks, desperate to maintain at least the idea of America's neutrality, were nervous of Nazi references in various drafts of the script. After Germany invaded Poland, Wanger, one of the more politically active members of Hollywood Jewry, decided to bypass the bank and raise the money on his own. He then approached Hitchcock. What, Wanger wanted to know, 'could Hitch do with this if he were given a free hand?'[65]

Although Sheean's book was stirring autobiography, there was nothing in it, according to Hitchcock, that was remotely filmic in terms of story and adventure. But that didn't stop him seeking out his old friend and collaborator Charles Bennett, who'd settled in Hollywood a couple of years earlier. Spurred on by Hitchcock, Bennett and Joan Harrison not to mention at least a dozen other uncredited writers worked on the screenplay which eventually boasted just four names including *Goodbye Mr Chips* author James Hilton and American humorist Robert Benchley. His authorly contribution was his own dialogue for a small but droll role as a rather boozy journalist. Hitchcock offered the eponymous lead to Gary Cooper who turned it down (he'd later regret his mistake) on the grounds the project was 'just a thriller'. So Joel McCrea was handed the part of a two-fisted newspaperman who after being sent off to Europe gets caught up in events presaging the outbreak of the Second World War. Not, you might think, unlike the set-up for *The 39 Steps*, which was indeed the model for much of which then unfolds in an authentically thrilling thriller full of Hitchcockian touches. These include enemy spies nesting in Dutch windmills, an assassination attempt atop Westminster Cathedral and a climactic plane crash into the sea.

Wanger was also extremely keen to keep the action as timely as possibly despite the fact that, like the banks, Hollywood was trying as far as possible to stick to the country's resolutely neutral stance. Though filming was actually taking place during the first half of 1940, the action of the film is meant to be set during the fortnight up to Britain's declaration of war on Germany on 3 September 1939. When Hitchcock returned from England after visiting his mother, with the premiere almost at hand, Wanger, having heard the director's tales about imminent bombing, demanded a new ending to reflect the impending threat. The result, penned by an uncredited Ben Hecht, is a stirring if shamelessly jingoistic coda as McCrea sits at a radio microphone and broadcasts to America from a London just beginning to suffer aerial bombardment from the Luftwaffe. With the national anthem welling up in the background, McCrea describes how death is coming to London and 'it feels as if the lights are all out everywhere – except in America'. 'Hang onto your lights,' McCrea implores his fellow Americans. 'They're the only lights left in the world.' Chillingly, five days after filming finished, the first German bombs actually fell on London.

According to John Russell Taylor, who wrote not just one of the best but also an authorised Hitchcock memoir, 'when asked about the conclusion now [in the 1970s] he is liable to back away from it, saying it was all the doing of Walter Wanger and Ben Hecht. But it is hard to believe that, in those very emotional days, he did not endorse it and find in it something very close to his own sentiments, even if left to himself, he would have hesitated to wear his heart so flagrantly on his sleeve.'[66] The following year, Hitchcock found *Foreign Correspondent* competing against *Rebecca* at the Academy Awards, specifically in three categories – Best Picture, Special Effects and Black-and-White Cinematography. It had six nominations in all but ended the evening empty-handed.

After *Foreign Correspondent*, Hitchcock juggled with various projects including *Forever and a Day*, an episodic flagwaver about a great British house and its various inhabitants down the years, and a thriller, *Before the Fact*, based on Francis Iles's novel which had long been on the stocks at RKO. While he passed on the first, the second was put on hold. Instead he succumbed to the not-inconsiderable charms of a pal, Carole Lombard, one of Hollywood's most popular blondes then married to Clark Gable, who begged him to make a film with her. The result was *Mr and Mrs Smith* (not to be remotely confused with an execrable 2005 film of the same name) in which she co-starred with Robert Montgomery. He was an after-, not to say last-minute, thought when, first, Cary Grant, then others turned down the 'Mr' part in this frothy comedy of a handsome, devoted yet gleefully warring couple. 'In a weak moment I accepted and I more or less followed Norman Krasna's screenplay. Since I really didn't understand the type of people who were portrayed in the film, all I did was to photograph the scenes as written,' Hitchcock would later confess.[67] Another of his biographers, Donald Spoto, suggests that this is perhaps being not so much as wise as rather churlish after the event since, at the time, he actually professed genuine enthusiasm for the assignment, explaining 'I want to direct a typical American comedy about typical Americans'.[68]

Though not quite as inconsequential as, say, *Waltzes from Vienna*, there is little to suggest in *Mr and Mrs Smith* the work of anyone but a mere hired hand. Yet it still managed to fool some critics like the reviewer in *Look* magazine, who trilled: 'The striking thing about this film is that Hitchcock has employed the same strategy that marks his blood-chilling melodrama … The net effect is the same, too – another Alfred Hitchcock hit.' It is also interesting to speculate whether the funny, feisty and fiercely intelligent Lombard might have become one of Hitchcock's favourite regular blondes had she not died in a plane crash aged 33 a year after her penultimate film. She certainly seemed to have a measure of the man judging by her jape on the first day of shooting. As he arrived on the set, he found a corral had been constructed with three sections, with a young cow inside

Cary Grant (1904–86), born Archibald Alexander Leach in Bristol, was the only child of poor parents. He set sail for the States in 1920 with an English comedy troupe where he settled eventually making his feature film debut as a Paramount contract player in *This is the Night* (1932). He shone in screwball comedy, romantic dramas, adventure and thrillers, often playing off his own film image. Twice nominated for the Best Actor Oscar – *Penny Serenade* (1941) and *None But the Lonely Heart* (1944) – he retired from the screen in 1966.

each one. Round their necks were ribbons with a disc marked, variously, 'Carole Lombard', 'Robert Montgomery' and 'Gene Raymond' (who was playing one of Mrs Smith's suitors). This was apparently a show-stopping rejoinder to Hitchcock's famously misquoted remark which had preceded him to Hollywood: that 'all actors are cattle'. At a Screen Producers Guild Dinner in 1965, not to mention numerous other occasions both before and after, he cleared up – or did he? – the infamous misunderstanding. 'My actor friends know I would never be capable of such a thought-less, rude and unfeeling remark … what I probably said was that actors should be *treated* like cattle.'[69]

Cary Grant who, like Hitchcock, was another kind of clichéd Englishman abroad as he plied his debonair trade in Hollywood, was a collaboration just waiting to happen. After declining *Mr and Mrs Smith*, Grant signed up for *Suspicion*, the revised title of *Before the Fact*, to play the charming but thieving and murderous husband of sweetly innocent Joan Fontaine. Gary Morecambe and Martin Sterling in *Cary Grant: In Name Only*, suggest, 'there had scarcely been a hint in any of Grant's performances of his suitability as a Hitchcock leading man but, in retrospect, it can be argued that there isn't a single leading male role in any Hitch-cock which Cary Grant could not have played and made his own.'[70] Grant would go on to star in three more of the director's films spread out across nearly 20 years, though never again in a part quite so ambiguous as Johnnie Aysgarth. In fact it was not so much ambiguous as downright crystal as originally authored and scripted.

Too much so for one of the RKO studio producers who, according to Hitchcock, re-edited the director's original version behind his back, deleting all possible references to Grant as a wife killer resulting in a version that ran a ludicrous 55 minutes.

Hitchcock's original ending had Grant poisoning his wife, little realising that he had unwittingly posted a letter from her to her mother in which he was unveiled as a killer. Studio chief George Schaefer, aware the new, abbreviated cut was quite absurd – not to mention unreleasable – allowed Hitchcock to concoct a revamped denouement. All kinds of new endings were mooted and as hastily discarded, from Grant joining the RAF

Cary Grant and Joan Fontaine pose with co-star Nigel Bruce in a promotional still for **Suspicion** *in 1941*

to Fontaine's suicide. Hitchcock later wrote 'I had to make the suspicion ultimately a figment of her imagination. The consensus was that audiences would not want to be told in the last few frames that as popular a personality as Cary Grant was a murderer, doomed to exposure.'[71] After more than 90 minutes of clear hints that Grant is a cold-blooded killer, he is finally revealed as nothing more than a bit of a bounder, conscience-stricken and even suicidal about his mounting debts but ultimately a loving husband whom Fontaine, despite being frightened within quite literally an inch of her life, is only too happy to welcome back to her bosom. 'Well, I'm not too pleased with the way *Suspicion* ends,' Hitchcock told Truffaut with some understatement.[72]

The new ending certainly paid off for Fontaine who in 1941 won the Best Actress Oscar that had eluded her the year before for *Rebecca*. Grant, who apparently approved of Hitchcock's original ending, was nominated as Best Actor ... but not for *Suspicion*, rather for his role as a grieving father in a tearjerker, *Penny Serenade*. In a vintage year of *Citizen Kane*, *Sergeant York*, *How Green Was My Valley*, *The Little Foxes* and *The Maltese Falcon*, Hitchcock's efforts also put the *Suspicion* in the frame for Best Picture. But there would be no cigar. He must have consoled himself with the fact that the film was a great success commercially and, for the most part, critically as well as sign-posting the future in the form of the single word title psychological thriller, which would punctuate his filmography over the next 30 years.

If *Suspicion*, like *Rebecca*, was set in some timeless, upper-middle class English universe (that was, of course, forever California) then *Saboteur*, which began filming soon after America had joined the war following the infamy of Pearl Harbor, swept Hitchcock right back to the front line of real life events. Still on loan-out from Selznick, he had come up with the idea of

fifth columnists sabotaging American defence plants into which
is woven the by-now rather familiar, very *39 Steps*, formula of a
wrongly-accused munitions worker on the run trying to clear
his name. There are even handcuffs and the inevitable blonde.
Though a little undermined by the rather lightweight B-movie
nature of his two leads, Robert Cummings and Priscilla Lane
(who were pale substitutes for the first choices, Gary Cooper and
Barbara Stanwyck), *Saboteur* is nevertheless a cracking, breathless
thriller with some set-pieces which rank alongside Hitchcock's

Inside the Statue of Liberty,
Robert Cummings closes in on
his adversary in the 1941 film
Saboteur

most memorable. Chief among these is the climax at the Statue of Liberty where our hero is pitted against the real saboteur, the weaselly Fry, played by stage actor Norman Lloyd in his feature film debut. After he got the role, Lloyd recalled being taken by Hitchcock to a bar across the road from Universal Studios. 'Hitch ordered a martini and I said I would have the same. When Hitch's "usual" arrived, it was in a goblet the size of those used to serve grapefruit, when the grapefruit is surrounded by ice. Mine, of course, was the same … The drink made me fear for my safety; on the other hand, I was afraid that if I didn't drink it, I might lose the part. I just sipped while Hitch drank one, then another. He was never drunk; it was his normal appetite.'[73]

Lloyd would certainly need all his wits about him for the Statue sequence on which he worked first, briefly, in New York with ace effects cameraman John Fulton before moving to Hollywood for the main part of the shooting. On Stage 12 at Universal were the hand, torch and balcony built to scale as well as the inside of the crown. Parallels had been built out to the balcony with mattresses. The scene ends with Fry dangling from the monument with his sleeve held from above by Cummings who is desperate to save him so he can establish his own innocence. Gradually the sleeve comes away and Fry plummets, screaming … Lloyd claims that Hitchcock felt the only problem with the sequence, 'which is technically supreme, was that story had the wrong man in jeopardy. It should have been the hero, he thought. He concluded that the scene on the hand of the statue, with all the technical and cinematic wizardry to hype up the audience, would have been more affecting had Bob Cummings been in jeopardy.'[74] Lloyd was also involved in another great Hitchcock moment, a real shoot-out at the Radio City Music Hall between him, Cummings and detectives while a gunfight is in noisy progress on the big screen. A man in the audience keels over after being shot with only the woman next to him aware of it. Said Lloyd: 'The essence of the Hitchcock touch in that sequence was not only the inter-mingling of reality, so to speak, with film, but also the humour of the situation, in which the audience continued to think all the shots being fired were on the screen; they were laughing; they were never aware of the real gun battle.'[75]

Perhaps because of the lack of more obvious star power, *Saboteur* tends now to be regarded rather unjustly as one of Hitch-cock's lesser efforts. Yet, not only are there some supreme thrills but also several blackly comic verbal gems, thanks in no small measure to the screenplay contribution by Dorothy Parker. Cummings and Lane are hiding out on a transcontinental train, which just happens to be transporting a circus. Stumbling into a carriage where the freaks are travelling, the pair are privy to an ongoing row between Siamese twins who'll only communicate through a third party. One says: 'I wish you'd tell her to do something about her insomnia. I do nothing but toss and turn all night!'

With such timely subject matter there was always a danger of life imitating art. As they filmed away in California, news came through that a French ship, the *Normandie*, being prepared to ferry troops, was ablaze and on its side in New York harbour … after probably being sabotaged. With an eye to the main chance, Hitchcock requested Universal's newsreel division to shoot some footage of the burning hulk. He then arranged for Lloyd to sit in the back of a mock-up of a cab and, when cued, look to his right with a slight smile as if glancing at the *Normandie*, somehow to suggest it was all his own handiwork. The brief juxtaposition of real and imagined was genuinely chilling, if perhaps a little too opportunistic for the US Navy who demanded (unsuccessfully) that the offending footage be cut from the final film. 'From a directorial point of view,' notes Lloyd, 'it shows a man who was really on his toes and aware of any opportunity to create something for his film: to take history at the moment and incorporate it into a script – in character, story and action.'[76] It also tends to belie Hitchcock's oft-repeated claim that because he had already laid out a script shot for shot, the actual shooting of the film was boring because it had all be done before in the script. So, spontaneity could after all play a part in Hitchcock's otherwise well-prepared universe.

Chapter 7

The Heat of Battle

During the gestation of *Saboteur* when it looked for a moment as if the film might be an RKO production, the urbane John Houseman, who'd worked alongside his Mercury Theatre co-founder Orson Welles on *Citizen Kane*, was instructed to exploit his Anglophilia and jolly Hitchcock along in the preparation of an original screenplay for the same studio. Houseman wrote in his autobiography, *Run-Through*: 'I had heard of him as a fat man given to scabrous jokes – a gourmet and an ostentatious connoisseur of fine wines. What I was unprepared for was a man of exaggeratedly delicate sensibilities, marked by a harsh Catholic education and the scars from a social system against which he was in perpetual revolt and which had left him suspicious and vulnerable, alternately docile and defiant. He was an entertaining and knowledgeable companion … But his passion was for his work, which he approached with an intelligence and an almost scientific clarity, to which I was unaccustomed in the theatre.'[77] What seems to have been an enjoyable collaboration, however, proved brief as the project switched to Universal. Although *Saboteur* was commercially successful, Hitchcock seems, in his own retrospect, to be rather harshly self-critical about what he perceived as its creative flaws: 'There was a mass of ideas, but they weren't sorted out in proper order; they weren't selected with sufficient care. I feel the whole thing should have been pruned and tightly edited long before the actual shooting. It goes to show that a mass of ideas, however good they are, is not sufficient to create a successful picture.'[78]

In those seemingly rare moments between filming and developing new projects – and enjoying legendary Hollywood restaurants like Chasens – the Hitchcocks were now determined to try and put down some roots in their adopted country. After two years in the rented house on Saint Cloud Road, they bought their first home just across Bel-Air Country Club's golf course on Bellagio Road, where he would remain for the rest of his life. Pat had happily settled in at nearby Marymount ('Preparing Young Women to Make a Better World') Catholic High School on Sunset Boulevard where she was an enthusiastic participant in school plays. With aspirations to become an actress, she even, aged 13, managed to win a part in a new play on Broadway. Unfortunately it ran less than three weeks and she was soon back at Marymount still nursing stage dreams. Not long after, Hitchcock also purchased a weekend place about 300 miles up the winding coast at Santa Cruz. Actually 'place' hardly does justice to the delightfully secluded property, built in the California-Spanish style and set amid 200 unspoilt acres near Monterey Bay.

The new retreat was quite some way south of the location of his next film, *Shadow of a Doubt*, set literally in the little Northern California town of Santa Rosa on Route 101 about 50 miles north of San Francisco, where suave Uncle Charlie has taken up residence at his sister's home. His favourite niece (Teresa Wright), called Charlie after him, gradually discovers that her namesake is none other than the notorious 'Merry Widow Murderer' currently being sought nationwide by the police. The basic idea for the film had come from the novelist husband of Selznick's story department head, Margaret McDonell. For his part, Hitchcock was very keen to work with Thornton Wilder, who'd previously had a hand in the 1940 screenplay of his own Pulitzer Prize-winning stage hit *Our Town*, and thought the writer would be the perfect man to fashion an intricate if slightly skewed view of small town American life. Like John Houseman, Joseph Cotten, who was cast as the ruthless serial killer, was another graduate of *Citizen Kane* who recalled, 'I cannot remember any shooting script that suffered so few alterations during production. All the actors agreed that the author's words were not only easy to learn, but a pleasure to speak.'[79]

In fact, Alma and Sally Benson also provided script contributions as well as an uncredited Patricia Collinge who penned at least one key scene in the final polish. Collinge, whom Hitchcock, had seen and admired on the London stage in the early 1920s, was officially on the payroll to play the sister and young Charlie's mother, who was named Emma after the director's own mother. Sadly, just a few weeks into production, as the cast and crew returned to Universal after shooting on location in Santa Rosa, old Emma died aged 78 on what would have been her 55th wedding anniversary. From that moment on, Donald Spoto suggests, the film was 'transformed … into a network of personal references. And the film is as much a key to the complexities of his inner life, and of his guilt, as it is to a network of meanings illustrating his relationships to his family, to his own divided self, and to the divided culture from which he had emigrated.'[80] If this seems like psycho-babble then John Russell Taylor adds an intriguing coda by pointing out Hitchcock's fascination with the proximity of evil ever since he was a teenager when there was a notorious poisoning near his home in Leytonstone. While *Shadow of a Doubt* is often cited as the director's own favourite among his films – something which he neither wholly confirmed nor ever completely denied – what Hitchcock genuinely relished, says Russell Taylor, was to chance again 'give the violence and menace in his films a local habitation and a name. Much of the effectiveness in his British thrillers had come from setting their extraordinary happenings against very humdrum, everyday sur-roundings. And, too, he was fascinated by the omnipresence of evil, the fact there was no refuge from it.'[81]

Unlike Cary Grant's Johnnie Aysgarth in *Suspicion*, there would be no re-write or redemption for Cotten's Uncle Charlie who suffers death by train just as he's trying violently to consign his niece to an equally loco-motivated fate. Cotten, who'd never played a killer before, let alone a serial version of that ilk, had sought advice from Hitchcock on the subject before shooting began. He was told 'Uncle Charlie feels no guilt at all. To him the elimination of his widows is a dedication, an important soci-ological contribution to civilisation … Forget trying to intellec-tualise about Uncle Charlie. Just be yourself … See you on the set, old bean.'[82]

Meanwhile, back at the war … Always game for a severe tech-nical challenge, Hitchcock had long been fascinated by the notion of making a film in the smallest possible space: minimum plot, maximum intensity. Like in a telephone box, for example. Or, what about a lifeboat adrift on the ocean after an Allied freighter has been torpedoed, as he suggested in a telegram to Ernest Hem-ingway? From Cuba, Hemingway passed, so Hitchcock turned instead to John Steinbeck, who rather half-heartedly contributed some material before quitting the project. *Lifeboat*, which still

The outrageous Tallulah Bankhead, one of Hitchcock's more unpredictable actresses, leers at him over lunch in Hollywood in 1943

88

bears the imprint of Steinbeck but was principally the work of the experienced screenwriter Jo Swerling, seems, in fact, to have been less about content and more to do simply with the challenge itself because, said Hitchcock, 'I wanted to prove a theory I had then. Analysing the psychological pictures that were being turned out, it seemed to me that, visually, eighty per cent of the footage was shot in close-ups or semi-close shots. Most likely it wasn't a conscious thing with most of the directors, but rather an instinctive need to come closer to the action.'[83]

There was content, of course, in an occasionally fascinating if preachy and ultimately rather stilted story reflecting, as Hitchcock wanted, a microcosm of war. Bobbing precariously in the Atlantic (actually the studio tank at 20th Century Fox), the lifeboat contains a cross-section of the world at war. Among the survivors are American seamen, including a black steward, an Englishwoman, the commander of the German U-boat that sank the freighter, and, presiding over this ocean-going powderkeg, a very worldly German-speaking American journalist. If you can chew scenery in such a claustrophobic, frankly unscenic, setting as this then Tallulah Bankhead, much better known for her flamboyant stage work than her relatively few screen appearances, managed it as the feisty hackette. Deliberately confrontational in her manner on and off set, she had a reputation for outrageous behaviour and it soon became known that she also had a penchant for discarding her undergarments during filming. Joseph Cotten was visiting Hitchcock on the set one day when he saw the cameraman go over to the director and whisper to him about Bankhead who, as the boat rocked back, moved backwards too with her legs wide open revealing her to be pants-less. Would Hitchcock have a word with her? The director told the cameraman to try the shot again and once more he reported back on the unacceptable visual. This time, said Cotten, 'Hitch lifted his stomach, stuck out his bottom lip and said, "This is not for me to handle. We shall call the hairdresser".'[84]

One of Hitchcock's more intriguing challenges on *Lifeboat* was to work out just how he could manage to effect his by now ritual cameo appearance in a film that palpably didn't have scope for his usual shtick as a passer-by or onlooker. Then it came to him. Following the recent, rather mysterious death – there was even some suggestion of suicide – of his brother William in London, Hitchcock began to have vivid intimations of his own mortality probably compounded by the fact he was hugely obese. So he decided to go on a crash diet in attempt to shed at least seven stone from his present mountainous 21 stone. He then recorded his loss in the form of 'before' and 'after' shots to appear on an ad, for a fake product called Reduco, in a crumpled newspaper found on the lifeboat. Year later, he said: 'As you know I still remain a prisoner of the old image. They say that inside every fat man is a thin man desperately trying to get out. Now you know that the thin man is the real Alfred Hitchcock.'[85] Although *Lifeboat* earned him his second Oscar nomination for Best Director, the film was, to all intents and purposes, Hitchcock's first Hollywood flop. The reason, opines Joel Finler, was as much timing as content. 'He had spent almost exactly a year on the film, which he was meant to complete in half that time. It would have undoubtedly done better if completed and released earlier in the war, in 1943 rather than 1944 when the tide of war was already swinging strongly in the Allies' favour; and by this time, movie audiences had also been subjected to rather too many war pictures.'[86]

Selznick, who always remained extremely proprietorial about his contractees even during his leave of absence as an active producer – Hitchcock was described rather peremptorily as 'one of my people' in a memo – eventually hooked up again with the director on a proposed adaptation of Francis Beeding's novel's *The House of Dr Edwardes*. But before tackling the assignment, Hitchcock was determined to try and become much more overtly hands-on with the war effort – a commercial for War Bonds featuring Jennifer Jones barely counted – to which end he flew home to England and put himself in the hands of his old friend Sidney (much later Lord) Bernstein who was films advisor to the Ministry of Information. Exactly the same age as Hitchcock, they first met back in the 1920s when Bernstein, born a few miles east of Leytonstone in Ilford, was a founder member of the Film Society and like Hitchcock on its Council. For the next few months Hitchcock lived at Claridges and commuted to Welwyn Studios where, ironically, one of his old bosses, John Maxwell, was now based after Elstree had been commandeered by the War Office. The result was *Bon Voyage* and *Aventure Malgache*, a couple of short propaganda films designed to vaunt the achievements of the French Resistance. Of the second, one critic noted, 'the most tedious 35 minutes in the entire Hitchcock canon. There is no suspense, no involvement in the activities of the characters, and a plot so limp that it's barely noticeable.'[87]

'The more I look at the dream sequence in *Spellbound* [the new title for *The House of Dr Edwardes*] , the worse I feel it to be. It is not Dali's fault, for his work is much finer and much better than I ever thought it would be. It is the photography, setups, lighting, et cetera, all of which are completely lacking in imagination …'[88] This Selznick memo, dated 25 October 1944, was to Daniel O'Shea, his executive vice president and general manager, and filed after the completion of principal photography. Urging 'a whole new shake'[89] on the sequence, Selznick, who'd later boast he'd only had to come on the set twice during

Ingrid Bergman in a moment of high anxiety in Hitchcock's masterpiece of suspense, Notorious, *1946*

Ingrid Bergman (1915–82) was invited to Hollywood by David O Selznick to film a remake of the romantic drama *Intermezzo* which had been her screen breakthrough three years earlier in her native Sweden. After hit roles in films like *Casablanca* (1942), *For Whom the Bell Tolls* (1943), *Gaslight* (1944), *The Bells of St Mary's* (1945) and *Joan of Arc* (1948) her career went into a tailspin when she left her husband for Italian director Roberto Rossellini. Effectively barred from American films for seven years, she eventually returned in triumph to win two more Oscars in *Anastasia* (1956) and *Murder on the Orient Express* (1974).

actual filming, was clearly making up for lost time. Especially now that Hitchcock, to Selznick's evident annoyance, decided to exercise a contract option and take a three-month holiday, had headed back to England. 'Dali' was, of course, the eccentric Spanish surrealist Salvador Dali whom Hitchcock had hired to design a key dream sequence in the story of a supposed madman who might, with some twists on the great tradition, have taken over the asylum. To that date, Dali's most notorious cinematic contributions had been as collaborator, nearly 15 years earlier, with director Luis Bunuel on the featurette, *L'Age d'Or* and the short, *Un Chien Andalou*, of, respectively, toe-sucking and eye-slicing fame. Out of respect to Hitchcock, Selznick reluctantly agreed to Dali. Hitchcock said 'He probably thought I wanted his collaboration for publicity purposes. The real reason was that I wanted to convey the dreams with great visual sharpness and clarity, sharper than the film itself.'[90]

Hitchcock must have reasonably figured that having Dali involved might at least add some extra flair, not to say, a little gravitas to what was otherwise, he later admitted, 'just another manhunt story wrapped up in pseudo-psychoanalysis'.[91] He also much later told John Russell Taylor in answer to a question about which other directors he rated, 'Oh, Bunuel. He's the master of us all'. With Dali on board, perhaps Bunuel's mastery might rub off on him. Hitchcock had begun working on the screenplay back in England with Angus MacPhail, the MacGuffin man, but it wasn't until he was back in Hollywood and in tandem with Ben Hecht, an advocate of psychoanalysis, that the film began properly to take shape. For Selznick, the film was much more about star power, in particular a pair of juicy roles for his own contract players, Ingrid Bergman, already an Oscar-winner for *Gaslight*, and Gregory Peck, in just his third film. Dali's skills were required to visualise the mental torment of Peck, as an amnesiac with residual guilt about the accidental death of his brother in childhood, who may have murdered the real Dr Edwardes. Hitchcock would have preferred the sequence to have been shot outdoors in full sunshine for sharpness' sake, but instead it was mounted on Selznick's own studio stages at Culver City.

Before the producer got his hands on it in post-production, there was 20 solid minutes of bizarre Dali imagery, including Bergman's character as a kind of Greek statue with an arrow through her neck and, with self-referential if less stomach-churning echoes of *Un Chien Andalou*, a giant eyeball menaced by scissors. 'Wonderful … belongs in a museum,' enthused Bergman, playing a shrink who falls for Peck.[92] Selznick clearly thought that as currently constituted a museum was indeed the best place for Dali's contribution. Some re-shooting and extensive editing resulted in four separate bits of the dream, just minutes here and there to punctuate memorably a less-than-convincing romantic melodrama, not so much underpinned as overscored by Miklos Rosza's aggressively lush soundtrack. The composer, competing against his own, and much subtler, music for *The Lost Weekend* was, ironically, the film's only Oscar winner from six nominations in all, including Best Picture and Director, making it Hitchcock's third unsuccessful 'nod' since he'd arrived in Hollywood. Academy Award recognition or not, John Russell Taylor has convincingly suggested that the film marked Hitchcock's 'definitive absorption into the American cinema.' Up till then he was somehow always the outsider looking in. 'From *Spellbound* on that all changes – Hitch has become, quite simply, an American film-maker.'[93] This so-called 'Americanisation' of Hitchcock also resulted in, dollar for dollar, one of his biggest box-office hits and a new kind of accolade which could only add to his public standing – above-the-title billing, as in 'Alfred Hitchcock's *Spellbound*'.

The war, which had still been raging throughout the production of *Spellbound*, was finally over by the time Hitchcock began shooting his next film which, at first glance, smacked, in personnel terms anyway of *déjà vu* – himself, Selznick, Ben Hecht and Ingrid Bergman – while also touching on recent hostilities in a quite remarkably timely way. Selznick had long filed away a short story from the *Saturday Evening Post* by John Taintor Foote about a young woman recruited by government to obtain crucial information by sleeping with a suspected spy. During filming on *Spellbound*, he passed it on to Hitchcock who spotted immediate potential and started sketching out ideas with Hecht. While Hitchcock was much taken with playing up the angle of a woman ruthlessly exploiting her sex to gain information, Hecht seemed to be more interested in the spy element. The resulting screenplay, *Notorious*, was a glossily effective mixture of both. Then, with the all the elements in place, including Cary Grant, as the intelligence agent who uses Bergman to help uncover a nest of Nazi spies, Selznick, now up to his memos in *Duel in the Sun*, sold the project, lock, stock and half of the profits, to RKO. Despite this, he'd later note, surely a shade fancifully, 'Notorious was entirely my conception. I did the script with Hitchcock and Ben Hecht, prepared it for Ingrid Bergman [he apparently actually wanted Vivien Leigh] and Cary Grant, and then sold the entire package to RKO, where Hitchcock not only continued with the direction, but took over from me as producer. So I have never included that in my productions, although I was responsible for the whole project.'[94]

Selznick had also been particularly lukewarm about one of Hitchcock's more inspired sub-plots – his celebrated MacGuffin here – in which Grant and Bergman, now married to the suspected Nazi, discover uranium stashed in her spouse's wine bottles. Before *Notorious* began shooting – and, remember, this was months before America dropped the A-bombs on Japan – Hitchcock and Hecht visited one of the country's top scientists at CalTech who firmly pooh-poohed, presumably for the best security reasons, their leading questions about uranium and bomb-

Hitchcock and Ingrid Bergman on the set of Spellbound

making. The story then goes that the FBI had Hitchcock, who seems to have stumbled on one of the greatest scientific secrets of the 20th century, under surveillance for the next three months.

It was also maybe something of a surprise that Grant had been pressed back into service again, as the mysterious T R Devlin, since he seems to have been less than pleased with the way he perceived he'd been treated on *Suspicion*. He had never liked Joan

Fontaine anyway and he always felt that Hitchcock had favoured her in his direction to his own detriment. But if there was any undercurrent, that doesn't seem to have been apparent during a trouble-free shoot. While there is no doubt that Bergman enjoyed very close attention indeed from the director – some biographers have even suggested he carried a serious, if unrequited, torch for the Swedish-born actress – Grant was never knowingly neglected either. Indeed, in a film full of moral ambiguity, the actor, at once heartless and loving, tapped into a dark side he hadn't fully displayed before or since. Gary Morecambe and Martin Sterling wrote: 'The doubts and insecurities that usually lay beneath the urbane exterior of Grant were laid bare in the film. Alfred Hitchcock's genius was to see what lay beneath and to expose it. But then Hitchcock, more than any other director, found it easy to recognise Grant's insecurities. They were, after all, his own.'[95] While Bergman aroused, according to Donald Spoto, 'the unrealised and misshapen, adolescent romantic impulses of a lovesick middle-aged director towards an unapproachable goddess,'[96] there's a strong argument for suggesting that Grant was everything that Hitchcock longed to be: tall, slim, good-looking, even sexually ambiguous. Reflecting, 20 years later, on matters of size and those trademark cameo appearances, Hitchcock joked about what might have been his possible fate had he been a passenger in *Lifeboat*. Then he added, with perhaps something more than just wishful thinking: 'You may be sure that in securing an actor for my next picture, I was more careful, I gave casting an accurate and detailed description of my true self. Casting did an expert job. The result: Cary Grant in *Notorious*.'[97]

Apart from a cinematographic echo of *Young and Innocent* in which the camera swoops from on high to a tight shot on Bergman's hand, the film's most talked-about visual is a record-

Cary Grant and Ingrid Bergman find their way around the censor's rules with a lengthy but interrupted kiss in **Notorious**

breaking screen kiss between her and Grant. There were, at the time, strict censorship guidelines dictating that no kiss could last more than three seconds. Hitchcock got round the restriction by having the couple kiss, then nibble, then talk and kiss again, holding each kiss no longer than three seconds as they moved from a balcony to indoors. The result was an extraordinarily erotic three *minutes*. If he couldn't have her then, the infatuated director might have reasoned, why not his fantasy *alter ego*?

Chapter 8

Matters of Technique

Notorious proved to be a smash hit, one of the quartet of Hitch-cock's biggest earners, along with *Spellbound* then, later, *Rear Window* and *Psycho*. However, Hitchcock, who'd also just enjoyed the comparative freedom of his first American producer credit, was now about to go back to his final contractual stint with Selznick. For his part, the perpetually cash-strapped Selznick had, as result of his sale to RKO, not only just missed out on 50 per cent of a lot but also probably sensed at the outset that Hitch-cock might have had his mind on other, and doubtless better, things than a rather hoary old English courtroom drama like *The Paradine Case*. To make matters even trickier for Hitchcock, there was a sense here that this particular project was more personal than usual. Even as far back as 1933, Selznick had been trum-peting his intentions to make a film version of Robert Hichens' novel co-starring John Barrymore, Lionel Barrymore and Diana Wynyard, as a woman on trial for murdering her blind husband. Hitchcock and Alma completed the first draft of the script before he successfully suggested bringing in the Scots playwright James Bridie to work on it. The fact is Selznick actually wanted to do the adaptation himself and his name is firmly on the credits. Said Hitchcock, rather dismissively, 'He would write a scene and send it down to the set every other day – a very poor method of work.'[98]

As if script problems weren't enough, the film proved fatally hamstrung by the casting of at least two of its three Selznick contract players – Gregory Peck, unlikely as a lovelorn English barrister, and the suave Louis Jourdan, meant to be a horny-handed son of the soil. However, the third, Alida Valli, like Jourdan in her first Hollywood film, proved a suitably alluring *femme fatale* although Hitchcock had briefly harboured hopes of luring Greta Garbo out of retirement for the role. Then there was Charles Laughton as the judge, re-united with his director for the first time since their unhappy experience together on *Jamaica Inn*. This time round, Laughton was neither producer nor top-of-the-bill, while Hitchcock, more concerned with the inadequacies of other members of the cast and the implausibilities of a creaking script, tried, but mostly failed, to paper over the cracks with the odd moment of technical virtuosity. Selznick's concerns about Hitchcock and the film's slow rate of progress during shooting were spelt out in a 'Confidential' memo to O'Shea and Ernest Scanlon, his company treasurer, on 28 December 1946. Selznick wrote: 'I think he has rather sensed our seeming indifference to cost, and the lack of a firm hand, which I at least once applied with him, and an indifference to costs and time, which disappoint me greatly and which I think must be attributable to us, in view of what we have seen and what we know of his extraordinary efficiency when he wants to be efficient … He told me tonight that he thought it was disgraceful the way we went into this picture with the physical production – photography, sound etc – *twenty years behind the times*.'[99]

After 92 days in production with its budget soaring to $4 million, almost twice as much as either *Spellbound* or *Notorious*, *The Paradine Case* proved to be, noted Joel Finler, 'if inflation is taken into account … the most expensive film of Hitchcock's entire career.'[100] Had it also followed the box-office example of the previous two films, then the huge cost might then hardly have mattered. However, these Old Bailey melodramatics were eventually met with public indifference resulting in one of Hitchcock's three biggest commercial flops (the others were *Under Capricorn* in 1949 and *Topaz* in 1969).

Before, during and after filming, Hitchcock's mind was, as Selznick rightly suspected, indeed on other matters. In common with other top Hollywood filmmakers at the time such as John Ford, Frank Capra, George Stevens, Robert Rossen, William Wyler and Lewis Milestone, Hitchcock wanted to set up his own independent production company with much more personal control. Hatched during various visits to London, and in partnership with Sidney Bernstein (who with his brother Cecil also ran the burgeoning Granada chain of cinemas in the UK), Transatlantic Pictures officially came into being shortly before *The Paradine Case* began filming. As the company title suggested, the aim was to make films alternately in London and Hollywood and the first production, which started shooting in January 1948 was *Rope*. Patrick Hamilton's play, with homoerotic undertones, was first produced on the London stage in 1929 and concerned a couple of arrogant Oxford undergraduates who conceive and carry out 'the perfect murder' of a fellow student. Hamilton always denied his 'inspiration' was the 1924 true-life Leopold-Loeb 'thrill killing'. Hitchcock, who apparently had previously planned a film version in the 1930s, was now principally interested in the subject matter

– Americanised by Arthur Laurents and actor Hume Cronyn – as '… a stunt'.[101]

The play, called *Rope's End* in the States, had been played out in real time with the action confined to a single claustrophobic setting and Hitchcock wanted, in a much more drastic refinement of, say, *Lifeboat*, to try and find a cinematic equivalent of this suspenseful immediacy. For his first film in colour, he decided to shoot it in sequence, on an elaborate set in Warner Brothers' studio at Burbank, in a series of continuous so-called 10-minute (the length of a single camera roll) takes with minimal editing because, to Hitchcock, it was effectively pre-cut. Talking about the film just months after he'd finished shooting, Hitchcock could barely conceal his pleasure in taking on what he described as 'my most exciting picture … until *Rope* came along, I had been unable to give full rein to my notion that a camera could photograph one complete reel at a time, gobbling up 11 pages of dialogue on each shot, devouring action like a giant steam shovel'.[102]

With the benefit of hindsight, he was considerably more circumspect, especially when it came to a question of more judicious editing. He told Truffaut that the idea of a 'single shot' narrative was 'quite nonsensical because I was breaking with my own theories on the importance of cutting and montage for the visual narration of a story … no doubt about it, films must be cut'.[103] Although Hitchcock claimed that filming continuous action somehow sustained the mood of the actors, the reality for his long-suffering troupe seemed that the director's self-styled 'stunt' was more a case of the dubious triumph of style over substance or, for that matter, sense. James Stewart, in the first of what would be four starring roles for Hitchcock, played the murderous students' one-time housemaster whose theories

After completing the filming of Under Capricorn *in Britain, Hitchcock was photographed by* Picture Post *showing Ingrid Bergman around London*

may have unwittingly ignited their monstrous deed. In an 80-minute cat-and-mouse game set in a fancy New York apartment, the teacher turns detective as he literally lifts the lid on their crime. However, according to one of his co-stars, Farley Granger, as the more reluctant half of the homicidal duo, Stewart 'never really got comfortable with the idea of playing this real heavy, this true villain. After all, no matter what he says at the end, his is the character that has triggered the killing in the story. He was extremely conscious of being this dark figure, and that made him edgy all the way through.'[104] Hitchcock would make light of the fact that Stewart endured sleepless nights during filming, which, he claimed, was less about the actual role and more to do with attempting to cope within the meticulously rehearsed technique which, the director admitted, was 'bewildering',[105] involving an almost constantly roving camera on a set where, in an instant, walls or even furniture might have to be 'wild' (moved to one side or be whisked away out of shot).

Audiences, however, proved to be less than wild about Hitchcock's 'stunt' that was, at its best, simply a rather gimmicky-photographed stage play. For the director, it was, in the final analysis, a 'miracle of cueing'.[106] The second, and last, film in his Transatlantic arrangement would have needed more than a miracle to surmount the problems of a production which despite the best technical intentions seemed to conjure up the bad old period days of *Jamaica Inn*. As if to compound the felony, Hitchcock was back (not counting the two war-time shorts) film-making on English soil for the first time since that salty schlock just before the war. The *raison d'être* for *Under Capricorn*, an absurdly overheated romantic melodrama of murder and incipient madness set in 1830 Sydney, seems to have been purely a chance for Hitchcock to show off his star Ingrid Bergman; that

he, the freshly independent British filmmaker, was now returning home with the biggest international star in the world by his
side. It was, he admitted, 'stupid and juvenile'.[107] As it transpired,
it appears that his return was less than triumphal. According
to Donald Spoto, it was 'greeted with alarming chilliness; his
absence during the war still angered many in English cultural
and social life'.[108] Although Hitchcock still revelled in his British
status, the press were well aware that both his wife and daughter
had taken American citizenship.

*Ingrid Bergman was the most
famous and adored actress
through the 1940s. Hitchcock
was captivated by her beauty
and cast her in three of his films*

As well as serious script problems, for Bergman in her third and last film for the still-besotted director there was also, as James Stewart could have warned her, Hitchcock's continuing obsession with visual technique to contend with. For, while giving himself much more scope for editing, he was still determined to try and refine his long-takes *Rope* experiment. Lighting cameraman Jack Cardiff, who'd last worked with Hitchcock as a 'numbers boy' on *The Skin Game*, recalled, 'With *Under Capricorn*, it wasn't quite that bad, but it was still largely one-reel takes. It wasn't that every single shot was 10 minutes, but every few shots were 10 minutes or eight minutes long.'[109] However, what might have, in principle, perfectly suited *Rope*'s single setting was quite another matter when it came to filming on several sets and even on different levels. Said Cardiff: 'We had an electric crane which could travel in any direction … without having to lay tracks. Joe Cotten [Bergman's co-star] told me one time that he was quite terrified of this bloody great electric crane, because it was quite quiet on these big tyres as it snaked around. He could just hear it at his back getting closer and closer and he was terrified he was going to be run over. It did come to rest once on Hitchcock's foot. I watched him and he was in agony, but he didn't say anything until the shot was over.'[110]

There was, of course, never any question of location filming in Australia. After shooting at Elstree, where one of the biggest sets was covered in lush carpet borrowed from a chain of cinemas, it was then back to Warner Brothers' studio in Hollywood for some final scenes and sunny exteriors (precluded by England's foul weather). The effort hardly seemed worth the bother judging by the eventual reaction. 'Overlong and talky, with scant measure of the Alfred Hitchcock thriller tricks,' wrote *Variety*, while *The Hollywood Reporter* moaned that the audience had to wait for more than 100 minutes for the first thrill of the picture. Suspense and thrills can be contained in all kinds of clothing but *Under Capricorn* – or 'Under Cornycrap' as Cotten's slip of the tongue perceptively re-titled it – would be the last time that Hitchcock ever ventured outside a strictly contemporary setting for a genre he had begun to make his own.

Although Transatlantic Pictures went into abeyance after just two films – a third was mooted then postponed when it became clear that *Under Capricorn* was shaping to be a big a loss-maker following *Rope*'s tiny profit – Hitchcock's deal with Warners' was more than compensation as it generously offered him *carte blanche* with subject matter, writers and actors. *Stage Fright*, from the bestseller *Man Running*, by Selwyn Jepson (who had been principal recruiter for the Special Operations Executive during the war) had the director back on, surely, much firmer ground. A third the cost of *Under Capricorn, Stage Fright* wove an enjoyable, convoluted, if resolutely lightweight, story of a young man (Richard Todd) who appears to have been framed for a murder committed by his worldly mistress, actress Charlotte Inwood (Marlene Dietrich). In the great Hitchcock tradition, our man goes on the run, this time round in the company of an old friend, RADA student Eve Gill (Jane Wyman). The twist here is that Todd actually did it while Wyman, who starts out trying to help prove him not guilty actually begins to fall for the handsome inspector (Michael Wilding) in charge of the case. For Hitchcock, the 'whodunit' element was secondary to what he described as a 'story of the theatre. What specifically appealed to me was the idea that the girl who dreams of becoming an actress will be led by circumstances to play a real-life role by posing as someone else in order to smoke out a criminal'.[111]

Hitchcock's pleasure in securing Dietrich seems to have been

Marlene Dietrich and Jane Wyman share a cigarette in a scene from Stage Fright. *It is not difficult to understand the animosity Wyman felt towards her glamorous co-star*

undermined by his disappointment with Wyman, who had arrived on the film as a recent Oscar-winner (for *Johnny Belinda*). Not only was she far too old, at 35, to play a drama student, but she regularly, and volubly, miffed at being so effortlessly out-glamourised by Dietrich who had Dior in her corner while she had to remain mousy. Todd, in reality five years her junior and nearly 20 years younger than his screen lover, was also just a bit dull despite the unexpected arc of his character. It must have been fun, though, for Hitchcock to have Pat, no stranger to his sets, actually in front of the camera for the first time. After her first short crack at Broadway some years earlier, she'd twice more been in abortive stage runs before her father had suggested, to her great delight, that she try out for RADA in London. She was still at drama school when he used her in the film both as a double for Wyman and, in a small role, as her pal Chubby Bannister. What the film lacked in humour from its younger leads was compensated for by some of the supporting actors like Alastair Sim, Miles Malleson and Joyce Grenfell who cheered things up on the fringes. And after the studied camera technique of the two previous films, Hitchcock used his camera with more restraint though at times with still dazzling results. He might have been rehearsing for *Frenzy* when he followed Todd through a door, upstairs and into Dietrich's bedroom in one, rather memorable continuous take. Then, with echoes of *Foreign Correspondent*, there was the elaborate staging of a decidedly damp garden party photographed through a sea of black umbrellas.

He did, however, commit, on his own admission, a couple of so-called cardinal sins of film-making with *Stage Fright*. The first was to lie in a flashback although, as Howard Maxford points out, 'in retrospect, this trick can be seen as the film's most effective device, perfectly setting up the deceptive plot, and effectively playing on an audience's expectations that flashbacks *do* tell the truth, especially when seemingly told by an innocent man wrongly accused of a crime, a contrivance already exploited to great effect by Hitchcock in the likes of *The 39 Steps* and *Young and Innocent*.'[112] The second and, said Hitchcock, 'the great weakness of the picture is that it breaks an unwritten law: the more successful the villain, the more successful the picture, and in this picture the villain was a flop!'[113] For the second picture running, he was based at Elstree Studios, one of his alma maters and now the home of BIP's successor, Associated British Pictures Corporation (ABPC), run by John Maxwell's protégé, Robert Clark, another dour Scot. It would be another five years before Hitchcock returned to England behind a camera, by which time he'd completed six more films, including two of his acknowledged classics, *Strangers on a Train* and *Rear Window*, and also become an American citizen.

Chapter 9

The American Way

Hitchcock's penchant for using great writers to help fashion his screenplays continued with *Strangers on a Train*, his first film back in Hollywood after his British sojourn which, wrote John Russell Taylor, 'had not exactly proved the unmitigated triumph he had hoped and fantasised it to be'.[114] Novelists and playwrights like Thornton Wilder, Robert Sherwood, John Steinbeck, Dorothy Parker, James Bridie, James Hilton, J B Priestley, Samson Raphaelson, and Ben Hecht had variously been through the mill with Hitchcock over the years. To adapt Patricia Highsmith's newly-published first novel, Hitchcock sought out 58-year-old Raymond Chandler, whose best-known creation, the world-weary private detective Philip Marlowe, had already appeared in films like *Farewell My Lovely* and *The Big Sleep*. From the start the collaboration proved problematic. Chandler preferred to work without interruption or interference, while Hitchcock was equally determined that he should be literally at the author's side during the preparation of his draft.

In a letter dated 17 August 1950 to his Hollywood agent Ray Stark, Chandler wrote: 'Hitchcock seems to be a very considerate and polite man, but he is full of little suggestions and ideas, which can have a cramping effect on a writer's initiative. You are in a position of a fighter who can't get set because he is continuously being kept off balance by short jabs. I don't complain about this at all. Hitchcock is a rather special kind of director, He is always ready to sacrifice dramatic logic (insofar as it exists) for the sake of a camera effect or mood effect. He is aware of this and accepts the handicap. He knows that in almost all of his pictures there is some point where the story ceases to make any sense whatsoever and becomes a chase, but he doesn't mind. This is very hard on a writer, especially on a writer who has any ideas of his own, because the writer not only has to make sense out of the foolish plot, if he can, but he has to do that and at the same time do it in such a way that any kind of camera shot or background shot that comes into Hitchcock's mind can be incorporated into it.'[115]

This 'silly story', as Chandler described it to his publisher, Hamish Hamilton, was actually the rather ingenious, diabolically twisty tale of a pair of young men who agree to 'swap' murders. Guy (Farley Granger) is to kill Bruno's (Robert Walker) disciplinarian father in exchange for the termination of his estranged wife who refuses to give him a divorce. Guy, who thought the initial arrangement was just a bad joke, is suddenly propelled into an escalating nightmare when the clearly psychotic, mother-fixated Bruno actually murders his wife and then demands the quid pro quo. Chandler was put on the payroll for five weeks after another writer, Whitfield Cook, had done an initial adaptation. On 27 September, Chandler wrote again to Stark: 'I haven't even spoken on the telephone to Hitchcock since 21 August when I began to write the screenplay, which was written in one day over five weeks. Not bad for a rather plodding sort of worker like myself. I don't know whether he likes it, or whether he thinks it stinks …'[116]

Judging by Hitchcock's subsequent instruction to Czenzi Ormonde, a one-time assistant of Hecht, who was signed up to write a new screenplay following Chandler's acrimonious departure from the project, the latter is more likely. A great fan of Chandler's, she asked to see what her hero had written expecting that she'd be required to do perhaps just a few revisions. Apparently Hitchcock picked up the great man's script, held it between thumb and forefinger and, rather theatrically, let it drop into the waste paper basket, saying, 'Now we start with page one.'[117] No, Hitchcock confirmed to Truffaut, he and Chandler's collaboration 'didn't work out at all', rationalising it thus: 'whenever I collaborate with a writer who, like myself, specialises in mystery, thriller or suspense, things don't seem to work out too well.'[118] The acrimony continued right on into the post-production phase when it came to the matter of apportioning screen credit. Hitchcock wanted Ormonde to have sole credit while the studio insisted, successfully, on Chandler sharing it with his name first. Another of the writer's letters provides yet more insight: '[Ray] Stark seemed to enjoy suggesting that my script was bad. But it wasn't bad. It was far better than what they finished with. It just had too much Chandler and not enough Hitchcock.'[119]

Hitchcock's subsequent reservations about the film weren't just confined to the script but also to what he rather harshly adjudged as 'the ineffectiveness of the two main actors'.[120] Granger, who'd played the weaker of the two killers in *Rope*, was perfectly effective here as the pretty-boy tennis player who gets caught up in events beyond his control, while Walker, up till then better known for his boy-next-door roles, was a revelation as the monstrous Bruno. A deeply troubled man in his private life, he died of a drugs overdose aged 32 just weeks after the film's premiere. Certainly Hitchcock seems to have had no criticism of his

'The fallacy of this operation was my being involved in it at all, because it is obvious to me now, and must have been obvious to many people long since, that a Hitchcock picture must be all Hitchcock. A script which shows any signs of a positive style must be obliterated or changed until it is quite innocuous, even if that means making it quite silly …'

RAYMOND CHANDLER

daughter Pat's brief-but-telling thespian contribution (as a suspicious sister) while he himself cheekily completed an unofficial musical trilogy, appearing with a double-bass after *Spellbound*'s violin and a cello in *The Paradine Case*. Hitchcock, who'd really wanted William Holden to play Guy, would prefer us to linger instead on some of his bravura set pieces – in particular, a brutal strangling reflected in a pair of glasses, a nail-biting tennis match and, most famously, Bruno's death in a spectacular fairground carousel crash.

Talking of first choices, Hitchcock had also originally wanted Montgomery Clift for the John Dall role in *Rope*, and he finally got his chance to employ the star three years on in his next film, *I Confess*, the first and only project on which the director's Catholic upbringing and the film's subject matter directly coincided. By the time Hitchcock got him, the actor's notorious insecurities were in full cry and this was a collaboration which proved not to be made in heaven. From a 1902 play by Paul Anthelme called *Nos Deux Consciences*, the project, like *Rope*, had been in the back of Hitchcock's mind since the 1930s when it had also been the unlikely basis for, of all things, a screwball comedy (*True Confession*, co-starring Carole Lombard and Fred MacMurray). Hitchcock's fascination with the material, a much-imitated premise, certainly wasn't to do with any comic possibilities. A German refugee confesses a murder to a Catholic priest, who because of his vow of silence subsequently becomes the prime suspect and has inordinate difficulty trying to clear himself without compromising his religious pledge. Clift loved the idea of playing a priest and he even booked into a monastery outside Quebec (where filming was due to take place) for a week to prepare for his role as Father Michael Logan. But that was where the fun stopped. First, George Tabori, one of the credited screenwriters, quit angrily

Hitchcock and his daughter Patricia on the set of Strangers on a Train

117

when Hitchcock changed his ending to have Father Logan live. This had been done it seems 'to placate the local diocese which was threatening not to co-operate with the film … [so] the priest is acquitted on grounds of reasonable doubt before being fully vindicated by the German's admission of guilt.'[121] Then, two weeks before start of shooting, the Swedish actress Anita Bjork, who was playing the female lead, was fired by Warner's. She'd arrived in America with her lover and their child in tow which was simply too much for the prudish climate of the time and she was swiftly replaced by the altogether more wholesome Anne Baxter, to Hitchcock's obvious disquiet.

Then there was neurotic Clift himself, from the 'Method' school of acting which Hitchcock instinctively distrusted, with his ever-present coach Mira Rostova – 'my artistic conscience' – by his side. 'Poor Monty was so disturbed and unhappy but Hitchcock never talked to him. He had the assistant director Don Page handle everything,' recalled Baxter.[122] Without even the director to hold his hand, Clift climbed further and further into the bottle. Said Baxter: 'Monty was so confused and removed from what was going on that sometimes his eyes wouldn't focus … We had to do important dialogue on the Lévis ferry, and I was to look lovingly at him while baring my soul. To do that I needed something, some response from him. But there was nothing, just a blank and distant gaze, and I had to imagine a look on his face.'[123]

Hitchcock, who earlier that same year had given Pat away in marriage to the grand-nephew of a Cardinal Archbishop at New York's St Patrick's Cathedral, later asked François Truffaut: 'Do you feel that there's a connection between my Jesuit upbringing and the heavy-handedness of *I Confess*?'[124] Truffaut, the former *Cahiers du Cinema* critic and, at the time of this query already

director of *Nouvelle Vague* treats like *The 400 Blows* and *Jules et Jim*, ascribed it instead politely to 'the austerity of the Canadian climate, which is further weighed down by the Teutonic gravity of Otto Keller [the killer] and his wife.'[125] Not even Truffaut's considerate equivocation would placate Hitchcock who claimed the real problem with the film was that apart from fellow Catholics, no-one else would relate to the film's crucial idea: the sanctity

Hitchcock inspects Montgomery Clift's uniform for flashback scenes on the set of **I Confess**

of the confessional. No, he avowed to his surrogate confessor, 'we shouldn't have made the picture'.[126] Hitchcock is too hard on himself and a film, in which the acting, for a change, stays longer in the mind than any visual trickery. Clift's authentic inner agony is perfect for the role while O E Hasse is probably among the best-ever Hitchcock villains. In his second film for the director following *Strangers on a Train*, for which he received an Oscar nomination, Robert Burks' monochrome cinematography in and around then streets of Quebec is never less than stunning. He would collaborate on a dozen films in all for the director, just pipping Jack Cox as the director's staunchest cinematographic sidekick.

I Confess actually managed to turn a small profit but enjoyed nothing like the acclaim of the earlier film which had, after Hitchcock's patchy period overseas, helped firmly re-instate him back in the Hollywood pantheon. However, after that pair of complex *noir*-ish thrillers, he next decided to play it absolutely safe. Warner's had already bought the rights to Frederick Knott's play, *Dial M for Murder*, which was transmitted as a live drama on the BBC in 1952, the same year it also became a huge stage success in London and on Broadway. After the comparatively wide open spaces of the previous films, this was straight back to *Lifeboat* country with almost all the action, apart from the odd scene, set in the London living room of married couple Tony and Margot Wendice. A cash-strapped ex-tennis pro, he suspects his rich wife of having an affair so plans the 'perfect murder' to protect his meal ticket. From the start, Hitchcock seemed to be clear in his mind that this was simply going to be a photographed stage play, despite the fact the expression tends to be used pejoratively by critics. Why bother, he reasoned, to 'open up' a play purely for the sake of it as so many other films had done? 'All we can do is

Grace Kelly and Ray Milland get close in a scene from Dial M for Murder, *1954*

120

take the audience out of the orchestra and put them on the stage with the players,' he once explained, in his defence of a well-constructed play which he reckoned could happily withstand transition between mediums with the minimum of interference.[127]

For their part, Warner's plan was to try and do that rather more literally than Hitchcock later intended, by utilising the gimmicky process of 3-D which they'd had some success with in 1953 for their horror film, *House of Wax*. Hitchcock, never one usually to shy away from innovation, found the extra technical demands of a huge and rather immobile camera restrictive and often frustrating. His main compensation came with the casting of Grace Kelly, who succeeded Bergman as his favourite leading lady but without the subtextual baggage. Asked why this particular gentleman seemed to prefer blondes, Hitchcock told *The Hollywood Reporter*, 'It is important to distinguish between the big, bosomy blonde who flaunts her sex and the ladylike blonde with the touch of elegance, whose sex must be discovered.'[128] For Hitchcock, who'd seen the 24-year-old in her first three screen roles (*Fourteen Hours*, *High Noon* and *Mogambo*) before casting her in his film, Kelly fell quite deliciously into the latter category. 'A woman of elegance will never cease to surprise you,' he purred.[129] The fact she was co-operative, funny and Catholic probably didn't hurt either. As the bemused wife of Ray Milland, who has blackmailed a seedy old school chum (Anthony Dawson) to kill her, she's not only beautiful but very touching. Kelly was, unsurprisingly, also the principal focus of perhaps the most elaborate 3-D sequence in the film, trying desperately while being strangled to reach out (towards us) for a pair of scissors in order to stab her vicious assailant. By the time the film was released in May 1954, the 3-D craze was over and the film mostly went out in a 'flat' version, effectively obviating all those technical hoops during production. Kelly told Donald Spoto, 'We all knew at the time that it would never be shown in 3-D. We knew it was a dying fad and the film would be released in the normal flat version, but this is what Mr Warner wanted.'[130]

What 'Mr Warner wanted' was no longer an issue when Hitchcock properly embarked on his next project which he'd already been sketching out while filming *Dial M for Murder*. His contract was officially up with the studio and his agent Lew Wasserman negotiated an astonishing new one for his client, now 53, across town at Paramount Pictures. The agreement called for Hitchcock to produce, direct and eventually own the rights to five films, starting out with *Rear Window*, an adaptation of Cornell Woolrich's 1942 short story, *It Had To Be Murder* (two years later re-titled *Rear Window* for a reprint). Bored with being confined to his bedroom during uncomfortably hot weather and unable to sleep, Hal Jeffries peers out on the 'rear-window dwellers' around him. Convinced he has spied murder committed by one of his neighbours, he tries unsuccessfully to convince his pals of the deed. It's only at the end we discover that Jeffries was immobile because of a broken leg. The premise, as confining as *Lifeboat*, *Rope* and *Dial M for Murder*, fascinated Hitchcock for its technical challenge as well as the chance to weave a series of small human stories in Jeffries' back-yard universe and to invent a love story for his new favourite actress, Grace Kelly. While Kelly, as the high society fiancée, was only too delighted to come on board, James Stewart, Hitchcock's choice to play disabled (from the outset) photographer L B 'Jeff' Jeffries – Kelly's rather unlikely amour – was much more wary especially as, on face value, it looked as if *Rear Window* could be a kind of *Rope* revisited. He seems to have been particularly reassured by the script, his first for Hitchcock by 34-year-old John Michael Hayes, already a veteran of radio drama. Stewart was also aware that the same subject had been worked on earlier by old friends, the agent Leland Hayward and the director Josh Logan, so the subject clearly had class.

While much has been made over the years about the film's theme of voyeurism and, in particular, Stewart's role as a 'peeping tom', Donald Spoto also suggests that Jeffries 'is clearly a Hitchcock surrogate in *Rear Window* … The character's wheelchair resembles the director's chair; with a long lens he spies on his neighbours; he gives them names and imagines little stories about their lives. Also like Hitchcock, he watches and admires, as a woman models a dress and a nightgown for him. She is a creature who arouses delight, but with whom, as the script insists, intimacy is threatening; looking and admiring is enough.'[131] Allegedly tying with *Shadow of a Doubt* as his own favourite film – despite not liking Franz Waxman's score – *Rear Window* is proudly held up by Hitchcock as an example of 'pure cinema' by which he really means the cinematic – 'the manipulative', some might call it – triumph of the visual over the spoken word. Despite what Hitchcock might think, the true success of *Rear Window*, in colour and for his first time in wide-screen, is the supreme mesh of all the film-making skills, most especially the script. There's a particularly poignant moment almost at the very end when the killer Thorwald (Raymond Burr) finally beards Jeffries in his own apartment – at the time, part of the largest set ever built at Paramount – and wails, 'What is it you want of me? Tell me what it is?'. It's been suggested with some justification he's the most sympathetic character in the piece, a whole lot more so than, say, Jeffries, the voyeuristic commitment-phobe. The film, a huge success, was nominated for four Academy Awards, including Direction but once again Hitchcock was passed over, this time in favour of Elia Kazan (*On The Waterfront*). Grace Kelly

did, however, win the Best Actress Oscar – but for *The Country Girl* and not *Rear Window*, for which she wasn't, like Stewart, even nominated.

The following year, Hitchcock, Hayes, whose *Rear Window* screenplay has also been nominated, and Kelly were re-united for *To Catch a Thief*, this time in the rather unexpected company of

Hitchcock photographed with Grace Kelly and James Stewart on the set of Rear Window. *At the time it was one of the largest sets ever constructed at a Hollywood studio*

Cary Grant, the director's other supposed *alter ego*. That Grant joined the cast and crew on location in the South of France was something of a surprise because two years earlier he'd announced his retirement. Now, just past 50, he was back for the third time with Hitchcock, claiming later, 'I really didn't want to do the film. I told Hitch that I was too old to play a leading man and that I was old-fashioned. It was only when Hitch told me that I would be playing opposite Grace Kelly that I did accept.'[132] Of course he was too old but, then again, Kelly was for the third time running cast opposite men old enough to be her father and no-one seemed to have noticed. If ever an actor could be deemed ageless it was of course Grant, who'd carry on as a kissing co-star with Eva Marie Saint, 20 years his junior, in *North By Northwest* and with Audrey Hepburn, half his age, in the thoroughly Hitchcockian *Charade* when he was on the cusp of 60. In *To Catch a Thief*, Grant was playing a retired gentleman cat burglar who, on this occasion, is wrongly accused of a spate of crimes along the Riviera. Kelly is the rich miss who helps him prove his innocence. Hitchcock's 41st film proved to be an expert romantic comedy-thriller with the emphasis more on the romance and comedy, with Oscar-winning cinematography by Robert Burks and a Hayes script (from David Dodge's novel) packed with juicy sexual innuendo. In *Writing with Hitchcock*, Hayes told Steven DeRosa that he wrote about a dozen different endings for the film. His personal favourite was a love scene between the two stars played out in Kelly's car high up on the Corniche overlooking Monte Carlo. They were to be so absorbed in their clinch that they only just noticed at the last minute her car is rolling towards the cliff edge. So then she asks him insouciantly to put his foot on the brake: 'He puts his foot on the brake and the bumper is just hanging over the edge, and I wanted to end there. But I couldn't

A publicity shot for Rear Window *reveals the allure of Grace Kelly, another of Hitchcock's favourite blondes*

convince Hitch to do it.'[133] Hitchcock, who admitted the story was lightweight and even a bit sentimental, told Truffaut, probably tongue in cheek, that the least he could do was try and avoid 'a completely happy ending. That is why I put in that scene by the tree, when Cary Grant agrees to marry Grace Kelly. It turns out that the mother-in-law will come to live with them, so the final note is pretty grim'.[134]

Kelly would, of course re-locate permanently to Monte Carlo two years later when she married Prince Rainier and, at the same time, retired from the screen. Film historian David Thomson wrote of the director-star collaboration: 'Who should play fairy godmother but Alfred Hitchcock. First he put her in a nightie and subjected her to Ray Milland's smiling trap in *Dial M for Murder*; next he used her to tease a James Stewart encased in plaster in *Rear Window*; finally he gave her Cary Grant to play with on the Prince's very doorstep in *To Catch a Thief*. In all three she was suggestive of high class (Hitchcock is always a snob) and her regal claiming of Grant for a goodnight kiss in a Monte Carlo hotel, or asking him to choose between breast and leg, are indelible …'[135] She remained friends with the Hitchcocks and in the early 1960s he even tried to persuade her out of retirement to star for him in *Marnie*. Her Serene Highness Princess Grace of Monaco died 20 years later on the same stretch of road where she'd filmed *To Catch a Thief*.

Chapter 10

Small is Beautiful

With *To Catch a Thief*, which proved a commercial hit despite receiving distinctly mixed reviews, Hitchcock had completed three films in 18 months, and even before he'd finished shooting it he was planning a fourth from a novel he'd first read four years earlier soon after its publication in 1949. Jack Trevor Story's *The Trouble with Harry*, about the discovery of a corpse, and how it resolutely refuses to remain buried, in a small English village, was described by a reader in Paramount's story department as 'an engagingly uninhibited little story, in a highly amusing style. The humour is too fragile and whimsical and the story too fanciful for transportation to the screen. Although the characters are presented as real people, they belong to a slightly fey world, and the plot itself it too tenuous for a screen comedy. Not recommended.'[136] Hitchcock had no such reservations as he put John Michael Hayes to work yet again, but apart from a transatlantic change of location – from Sparrowswick Heath to rural New England – his screenplay remained remarkably faithful to the original. There was even a rather nice hands-across-the-ocean connection with the casting of cuddly British character actor

Edmund Gwenn as Captain Wiles, whose actions trigger the black comedy. Gwenn, long a Hollywood resident, had previously appeared in three Hitchcock films, *The Skin Game*, *Waltzes from Vienna* and, in atypical mode, as the assassin who tries to push Joel McCrea off Westminster Cathedral in *Foreign Correspondent*. After a hat-trick of Grace Kelly performances, Hitchcock settled this time round on a young actress, in her first film, who could not have conformed less to the director's stereotype: 20-year-old, auburn-haired Shirley MacLaine. Very much part of an ensemble, her performance pleased Hitchcock although he was a little disconcerted by her habit of knowing everyone else's lines as well as her own. On her first day before the cameras, she was asked by the sound man how far she wanted to go with the first scene to which she replied, 'All of it.' He then proceeded noisily to lay out 15 pages of script around his sound equipment. When Hitchcock saw what was going on he laughed and told MacLaine that the usual practice was to shoot a few lines at a time!

Hitchcock liked the humour and, especially, the mood of the material. Mood, said Hitchcock, is apprehension. *The Trouble with Harry* had, for him, an element of 'murder by the babbling brook … Where did I lay the dead body? Among the most beautiful colours I could find … I wanted to take a nasty taste away by making the setting beautiful. I have sometimes been accused of building a film around an effect, but in my sort of film you often have to do that if you want to get something other than the cliché'.[137] Hitchcock's film is perhaps the nearest he ever came to an Ealing comedy of darker hue like *The Ladykillers* or *Kind Hearts and Coronets*. However, unlike them, it would probably be forgettable were it not for his decision to sign up Bernard Herrmann to compose the score. Herrmann was recommended to Hitchcock by Lyn Murray, who had written the

music for *To Catch a Thief*. Herrmann's music provided a lovely lyrical counterpoint to the rather uneven farce on screen and was to signal the beginning of one of Hitchcock's most important creative collaborations. As for the film itself, Hitchcock asked on the BBC arts programme *Monitor* in 1964 if he'd ever made a movie without regard to any audience, Hitchcock cited *The Trouble with Harry* more in sorrow than anger: 'It was a big loss … about half a million dollars. So that's an expensive self-indulgence.'[138]

The perfect Hitchcock casting for To Catch a Thief *, his favourite actors Grace Kelly and Cary Grant*

Bernard Herrmann (1911–75) was born in New York and educated at NYU and Juilliard. He scored many of Orson Welles's radio shows before turning to film with *Citizen Kane* (1941), the same year he won an Oscar for *The Devil and Daniel Webster*. Starting with *The Trouble with Harry*, Herrmann composed a further six films with Hitchcock – *The Man Who Knew Much* (in which he also appeared as the conductor), *The Wrong Man*, *Vertigo*, *North By Northwest*, *Psycho* and *The Birds*, as well as many of the director's TV shows. The pair had a disastrous falling-out during *Torn Curtain* when Herrmann was replaced.

Doris Day and James Stewart join Hitchcock at the premiere of his second version of The Man Who Knew Too Much, *1956*

Selznick had, back in the early 1940s, suggested to Hitchcock the idea of re-making *The Man Who Knew Too Much* with the Swiss and British locations replaced by Idaho, South America and New York before a cymbal-clashing climax at the Metropolitan Opera. But it remained just that, an idea for more than a decade before the director's thoughts eventually drifted back towards one of his career-making films of the 1930s. Always intending to hand over screenwriting duties to Hayes, Hitchcock worked first on the re-make with his MacGuffin man, Angus MacPhail, whom he'd known since the Gaumont-British days and with whom he'd collaborated on the two wartime shorts. As Hayes continued to work up their treatment into a script, Hitchcock had some other rather important business to conclude in Spring 1955. On 20 April, he was driven to the Los Angeles County Courthouse where, as one of a throng of ordinary civilians, he became an American citizen.

Later that same day, he met Doris Day to discuss her co-starring in his new film for which he'd already signed up James Stewart. On the face of it, the wholesome freckly Day seemed an unlikely 'Hitchcock blonde' but it turned out that he'd been a fan ever since seeing one of her rare dramatic performances as the wife of a Klansman in 1951's *Storm Warning*, and during a party at the time told her he was keen to use her in one of his films someday. The experience wasn't without its moments of high anxiety. Used to receiving suggestions and feedback about her performance, Day became concerned by Hitchcock's lack of interference, interpreting it as aloofness and even disapproval. She actually thought of walking off the film until she finally decided to confront him in his office. Why, she asked, wasn't he telling her what and what not to do. He told her mildly that she'd done nothing to be spoken to about, that everything she was doing was

right for the film and needed no further explanation. That was reassurance enough for her.

In one, hardly surprising, change among a number from the 1934 film, Day, who with her husband (Stewart) gets caught up in kidnap, murder and international intrigue while holidaying in Morocco, is a singer rather than a crack shot. Hence the chance to trill some Ray Evans and Jay Livingston songs including the Academy Award-winning 'Que Sera, Sera' ('Whatever will be, Will be'). Bernard Herrmann, on duty again as composer, was asked by Hitchcock if he wanted to write an original cantata for the Albert Hall sequence. He suggested they could do no better than go again with Arthur Benjamin's 'Storm Cloud' which Herrmann simply re-orchestrated, building up the music's crescendo to mask the near fatal assassination attempt. The film has its moments but not enough to justify the film's whopping two-hour running time (compared with the original's spare 76 minutes). Hitchcock's line about 'amateur' versus 'professional' in relation to the two versions could be re-interpreted as 'joyous' in 1934 compared with expensively 'going through the motions' in 1956.

The Man Who Knew Too Much also, sadly, signalled the rather abrupt end of the four-film collaboration between Hitchcock and Hayes. Their disagreement specifically arose over the eventual screen credit for the film (although there were money issues too). Hitchcock was anxious for Angus MacPhail to share it with Hayes so the American took the matter to arbitration with the Writers' Guild and won the sole credit. Steven DeRosa wrote: 'It was, in a sense, a mixed victory. Hayes knew the moment he challenged Hitchcock that there was no going back, that he had outgrown Hitchcock's ego, and that the partnership of Alfred Hitchcock and John Michael Hayes had been forever severed.'[139]

The film was still in post-production when the seal was finally put on Hitchcock as not just an above-the-title film-maker but also as one of the most potent brands in showbusiness at a time when merchandising was still in its infancy. On 2 October 1955, at 9.30 p.m., *Alfred Hitchcock Presents*, an anthology of suspense stories, started its run on the CBS network. For the first seven years, they enjoyed a half-hour format; for the next three, with the running length increased by 30 minutes, the show was logically re-titled *The Alfred Hitchcock Hour*. At a time when Hollywood was running scared of television and doing all it could with technical innovations – from Cinerama to Cinemascope – to try and counter the small-screen threat, the mainstream filmmaker Hitchcock's enthusiastic espousal of the dreaded rival was revolutionary. The idea came from his agent, Lew Wasserman of MCA (The Music Corporation of America), who thought that there was a way of capitalising on his client's larger-than-life shape and personality in the eager young medium. Both featured prominently in the way Hitchcock quickly took to TV. He named his production company Shamley Productions – after the old homestead – and made Joan Harrison its day-to-day producer with himself as a hands-on executive producer. When the show premiered with *Revenge*, directed by Hitchcock himself and starring his new protégée Vera Miles, the public was able just to gauge how Hitch-centric the format had been deliberately fashioned. The show opened with Gounod's 'Funeral March of a Marionette' over which a self-penned caricature of Hitchcock was superimposed before the man himself appeared on screen to deliver with, usually, mock solemnity an introduction to the story that was about to unfold.

Another key member of the television team was none other than Norman Lloyd, who'd toppled from the Statue of Liberty in *Saboteur* and been Ingrid Bergman's patient in the first ever scene Hitchcock shot with the actress on *Spellbound*. As well as being a distinguished actor, he was also a busy stage director and joined the Shamley team as associate producer. Before too long he was a regular on the roster of the show's directors along with the likes of Robert Stevens, Robert Stevenson, Don Weis, Justus Addiss and Herschel Daugherty. In the course of its long run, even better known names toiled in those 30- and 60-minute episodic vineyards – Robert Altman, Paul Henreid, Arthur Hiller, Sydney Pollack, Stuart Rosenberg, Ida Lupino and William Friedkin. Hitchcock directed 17 episodes in the short form, including such succulent titles as *The Perfect Crime*, *Lamb to the Slaughter* (from a Roald Dahl short story), *Poison*, *Banquo's Chair* and *Bang, You're Dead*, and one, *I Saw the Whole Thing*, in the longer format. His involvement in the show, for which Wasserman had structured a staggeringly lucrative financial deal including the personal retention of rights to each show after their initial broadcast, also made him a screen star in his own right. The public had always enjoyed those blink-and-you'll-miss trademark cameo appearances in his films; now he appeared before the TV camera in millions of American living rooms wittily topping and tailing a top-rated weekly show.

Most people probably thought that Hitchcock wrote his intros and outros himself. They were actually the work of Yale-educated James Allardice, a stage and TV writer, who was signed up by MCA to be Hitchcock's 'voice'. According to Norman Lloyd: 'The relationship was remarkable in that Jimmy Allardice found his perfect voice in Hitchcock; he said all of those wild things about the world through Hitch, who was willing to do any outlandish lead-in that Jimmy wrote. In a sense Jimmy was a part of Hitch's television persona. He wrote material based on

Hitchcock's personality and pushed it onto another level. Hitch would go to that level and make it even more outlandish – so that he would appear as his brother, Albert Hitchcock, as well as himself, or Jimmy would put Hitch inside a bottle, or have him wear golf knickers, or put him with a lion … Jimmy would have

Vera Miles became one of the actresses that Hitchcock put under contract. She would star in **The Wrong Man** *and join her sister Janet Leigh in* **Psycho**

him talk about his belly this way, his jowls that way, talk about his speech this way – and Hitch never blinked an eye. It made him very lovable to an audience; it made Hitch a major star of show business.'[140] It also made him very, very rich.

It was on television that he'd first spotted Vera Miles, in an episode of *Pepsi-Cola Playhouse*, and he seemed to think she had something of Bergman and Kelly about her. The younger sister of Janet Leigh, she had been a regular in Westerns before Hitchcock sought her out and put her under contract. For Hitchcock, the roots of *The Wrong Man*, her first feature film for him, probably go right back to those terrifying minutes spent in a police station in Leytonstone half a century earlier. Based on the true New York story of a musician (played by Henry Fonda) falsely accused of crimes he didn't commit, it's as much about the Kafkaesque spiral of legal red-tape from which he seems unable to disentangle himself. Hitchcock, who later claimed curiously 'it wasn't my kind of picture',[141] in fact does a very effective job, in what was probably the closest he ever came to drama-documentary, of creating a chilling, deliberately subjective portrait of an innocent man caught up in events beyond his control. The evidence seems circumstantial but it keeps piling up relentlessly against him. As his wife, Miles is very fine especially when driven to mental collapse by the case and confined to a sanatorium. In the original story, her character never properly recovered. On the studio's insistence, an epilogue was added to the film suggesting that she was eventually cured and the couple happily re-united.

Miles, for whom, it has been suggested, Hitchcock developed an unrequited passion as ardent as he'd had for Bergman, was also very much at the centre of his thoughts for his 45th production derived from a French thriller, *D'entre les morts* by Pierre Boileau and Thomas Narcejac. According to François Truffaut,

Hitchcock had been interested in one of their earlier novels, *Les Diaboliques*, a brilliantly twisty chiller, which was then turned into a Gallic film classic by Henri-Georges Clouzot in 1954. Spurred by his initial curiosity in their work, the authors then set out deliberately to write something which they thought would directly appeal to Hitchcock, although he claimed he never actually knew this was the history when Paramount offered him the project. However, trying to get a suitable script sorted for the subject, which became known as *Vertigo*, was a tortuous processes even by previous Hitchcock standards. He knew he wanted to re-locate the action to San Francisco and its environs and even had various sequences and sites in his head as he briefed various writers. Maxwell Anderson (who'd co-scripted *The Wrong Man* from his own documentary novel) and Alec Coppel came and went before Hitchcock, in between bouts of ill-health, turned to the playwright Samuel Taylor who had previously worked with Billy Wilder on the successful film adaptation of his own stage hit, *Sabrina Fair*. Hitchcock instructed Taylor not to read the source material but instead verbally mapped it out for him in scene-by-scene form. Taylor couldn't help noticing there was the small matter of a missing story to link those scenes, so together they began to paint characters and situations to bring those individual scenes alive. Superficially, the story concerns an acrophobic ex-cop who, forced to cope with guilt and his chronic fear of heights after failing to prevent the supposed suicide of an old pal's wife he'd been hired to tail, also becomes obsessed with a lookalike of the dead woman. 'I was intrigued by the hero's attempt to re-create the image of a dead woman through another one who's alive,' said Hitchcock.[142]

The finished script and film, suggests Spoto, 'bear everywhere the stamp of Hitchcock's deepest personal feelings – about himself,

Kim Novak and James Stewart in Vertigo. *Of all Hitchcock's films this is perhaps the one more than any other that still continues to cast a spell on cinemagoers*

about his idealised image of women, about the dangerous borders of emotional fixation, and about death, which is the romantic's ultimate obsession'.[143] The implication is that much of that was actually focused on Vera Miles who, allegedly, found the director's attentions occasionally too close for comfort. She'd taken time off during *The Wrong Man* to marry Gordon 'Tarzan' Scott, the second of three husbands, and then shortly before *Vertigo* was due to start shooting she had to pull out of the production because she was pregnant. With her wardrobe and final tests completed, the clearly irked Hitchcock apparently responded to this devastating news with the deeply uncharitable 'she should have taken a jungle pill'.[144] With James Stewart, in his fourth and last not to mention most complex role yet for the director, already signed up as the phobic, haunted Scottie Ferguson, Hitchcock turned reluctantly to Kim Novak as Miles' late replacement after Wasserman negotiated a loan-out from Columbia where she was contracted to its monstrous studio boss Harry Cohn. Her roles to date certainly didn't seem to suggest she was capable of the same kind of skill and emotional depth Miles had brought to something like *The Wrong Man*. But Hitchcock had reckoned without a different kind of motivation that Novak spotted in the dual roles of Madeleine Elster aka Judy Barton.

On the 40th anniversary re-issue of *Vertigo*, Novak explained: 'When I read the script I thought it was absolutely incredible. I thought my playing the role was obviously meant to be because it seemed to be so much of what I was going through already at Columbia. We'd be told: "You're special, you're different, we want you" and then someone else would say, "we want you but we want you to look like somebody else". I think playing that role in *Vertigo* really represented my desire to be heard, to have a voice as well as representing all the things that were happening to me. To tell you the truth, I never thought about whether it would be a great movie or not.'[145] Novak, who also brought to the film an almost otherworldly beauty – a 'carnal' quality, purred Truffaut – that the pretty but more homely Miles would never have achieved, was quick to give the lie to some reports that she and Hitchcock were endlessly at loggerheads during filming. 'All he was strict about was the definite ideas he had of the exterior of the character. Before I even met with him I met with [costume

Saul Bass (1920–96). Graphic artist, title designer and animator. Born in New York City, he enjoyed particularly fruitful collaborations with three directors, Otto Preminger, Hitchcock and, latterly, Martin Scorsese. After working on *Carmen Jones* (1954) and *The Man With the Golden Arm* (1956), Bass then also created logos and posters for other Preminger films such as *Anatomy of a Murder* (1959) and *Advise & Consent* (1962). Long after his distinctive trio for Hitchcock, he did the title designs for Scorsese's *Goodfellas* (1990), *Cape Fear* (1991), *The Age of Innocence* (1993) and *Casino* (1996). He won the Best Documentary Short Oscar in 1968 for *Why Man Creates*.

A publicity shot for **Vertigo** *illuminating Kim Novak's double role as Judy Barton and Madeleine Elster*

designer] Edith Head who showed me sketches of Madeleine's costumes. I asked her about the fabric and it was very stiff and I wondered how comfortable that would be because she wears it for much of the movie. I thought if it could be a softer fabric and feel a bit different I would feel better as an actress.'[146] Novak also wasn't too keen on some black shoes in her prospective wardrobe. Miss Head suggested she speak to Hitchcock about all this. According to Novak, the meeting was a rather surreal affair with her breathlessly explaining her objections as the director politely listened. After she'd finished, he thanked her for her interest but said she *would* wear what she'd been asked to. 'After that, I thought of it as a challenge. I had to make it work for me. I couldn't let it keep me from doing a good job. The stiff suit turned out to be a help too because I was playing a façade – somebody who was pretending to be someone else. It was like the discomfort of wearing someone else's clothes that you don't quite feel at home in, that you can't relax with. It was exactly the right feeling to have.'[147] Whatever reservations Hitchcock might have had residually about Novak weren't shared by his daughter who later said: 'I do think her performance is unbelievable because if you stop and think, she's not playing two parts – she's playing one character who's pretending to be another, which is much harder.'[148]

From Saul Bass' titles and Robert Burks' lush cinematography – dictated by Hitchcock's requirement for a red and green, stop-go, colour palette – to Bernard Herrmann's jagged score, *Vertigo* is a quite astonishing psychodrama. It is perhaps the one Hitchcock title that has, long after the director's death, soared in audience approval quite counter to its rather lukewarm appreciation by critics and crowds at the time. It is way too long, at times even a tad dull, yet it carries you along on a wave of its own neuroses, while prior knowledge of the director's own baggage adds a fascinating extra layer to this superior study in fixation. It's not difficult to understand how the achingly attractive – and on occasion bra-less – Novak could become a less than obscure object of desire to Stewart who, for his part, helped make sense out of a confused plot and was even, at times, bravely unsympathetic as the fearful Everyman. He thought his reward might be a role in Hitchcock's next film. Instead he was despatched to Columbia on far less terrifying duty to co-star in Novak's next film (*Bell, Book and Candle*) as a quid pro quo for her *Vertigo* secondment. His loss was Cary Grant's gain.

Chapter 11

Off the Compass

After juggling various working titles like 'In a Northwesterly Direction' and 'Breathless' (coincidentally, the film would be eventually released in the same year as Godard's nouvelle vague classic of the same name) and 'The Man in Lincoln's Nose', Hitchcock started directing *North By Northwest* as he entered his 60th year. His non-exclusive contract with Paramount meant he could work for other studios and while he was working on *Vertigo*, MGM approached him about doing a film version of Hammond Innes' nautical bestseller *The Wreck of the Mary Deare*. Thanks to an introduction from Bernard Herrmann, Hitchcock met up with screenwriter Ernest Lehman, who was contracted to Metro and, more importantly, they got on famously. Before too long, they were mutually cooling on the Innes project (later filmed by others) and instead hatching the idea of doing 'the Hitchcock picture to end all Hitchcock pictures'.[149] The chase theme was crucial and various sites in mind included the UN headquarters in New York and Mount Rushmore (with its Presidential heads) in South Dakota. But, according to Joel Finler, 'it came together more clearly when Hitchcock recalled an idea that had been offered to him by a New York newspaperman. What if the CIA had created a non-existent government agent as a decoy to divert the attention of some enemy spies away from the real agent, and the innocent hero happens to get mistaken for the decoy?'[150] And whatever James Stewart had thought, or been led to think, during the making of *Vertigo*, the project was planned always very much with Cary Grant – the more elegant and wish-fulfilling of Hitchcock's *alter egos* – in mind as the director's latest man-on-the-run.

The title may have come from *Hamlet* ('I am but mad north-northwest …') which, suggests critic Pauline Kael, is 'the clue to the mad geography and improbable plot. The compass seems to be spinning as the action hops all over the country and the wrong people rush about in the wrong directions.'[151] Odder still, Hitchcock had once actually planned to film a modern-dress version of the Shakespeare play back in the immediate post-war years and even had Grant in mind to play the melancholy prince. By the time the actor came to play Roger O Thornhill, perhaps the most put-upon of all Hitchcock's targeted heroes, he was, at 54, perhaps just a bit old for a student but being Grant, somehow still ageless. And not too old for romance with the director's latest icy-blonde Eva Marie Saint – the studio had wanted Cyd Charisse – who's dragged into the chase and ends up sharing a train berth with Grant as the third Mrs Thornhill.

"Never,' wrote Richard Schickel with a fair degree of psychological licence, 'did Hitchcock more brilliantly use comedy, romance and thrills to hide his true theme – the sadistic degradation of pride … The point of *North by Northwest* is to destroy Thornhill's arrogant innocence, strip him of the adult's artifice and illusion and to return him to the anxious state of a lonely child in a darkened room; to ask him to re-imagine himself

and re-imagine the world; to make of him, if you will, Archie Leach.'[152] It's even been suggested that the film was Hitchcock's deliberate 'assault' on the creation known as 'Cary Grant', a chance to draw a rather perverse parallel between the Bristolean who'd re-invented himself as a Hollywood star and his character in the film who may or may not be who he says he is. That blur, if blur there is, was intriguingly compounded in the film's original

Cary Grant menaced by a crop-sprayer in one of North by Northwest*'s most memorable scenes*

trailer which used the name 'Cary' rather than 'Roger' on the soundtrack to outline the jeopardy in store for him/the character. Grant told Hitchcock during shooting that he hadn't a clue what was going on. But then that's just what his character's meant to think – caught up in events beyond his control and on outlandish locations where anything could and did happen.

If ever actors could be considered simply props in Hitchcock's big picture, then that was surely the case here for two of the director's best-remembered and most oft-imitated sequences. Grant could well have been forgiven for thinking what on earth he was doing alone on the wide-open plains of America's Mid-West (actually, near Bakersfield, California) being buzzed by a crop duster plane. As a serious assassination attempt, it seemed to make no sense at all until you understood the director's motivation. We know Grant has been sent on a rendezvous with death. Hitchcock said: 'Now the cliché treatment would be to show him standing on the corner of a street in a pool of light. The cobbles are washed by the recent rains. Cut to a face peering out of a window. Cut to a black cat slithering along the bottom of a wall. I said *no*. I would do it in bright sunshine with no place to hide, in open prairie country. And what is the mood? A *sinister* mood. There's a not a sign of where the menace can come from, but eventually it turns up in the form of a crop duster airplane. Someone inside the plane shoots at Cary Grant and he has nowhere to hide.'[153] It's all about the set-piece however logically absurd it might be. 'It's obvious that the fantasy of the absurd is a key ingredient of your film-making formula,' Truffaut remarked to Hitchcock, while noting the scene is 'totally gratuitous'.[154] 'The fact is, I practise absurdity quite religiously,' retorted Hitchcock.[155] If Hitchcock had had his way, the climactic scene on Mount Rushmore, as Grant wrestles for his life with

the villainous James Mason, would have been even more delight-fully absurd. He'd wanted Grant to slide down Lincoln's nose, hide inside his nostril and then have a sneezing fit. None of this remotely amused the federal authorities, which not only refused permission to use the actual monument (apart from background shots) but also were very strict with what the filmmakers could recreate back at MGM Studios. Only the faces below chin level could be mocked-up, they ruled without a flicker.

Grant's face, as iconic as those US presidents' and probably better known then most, remains a picture throughout, alternately registering confusion and charm. As some critics noted, he seemed to have got younger and better-looking with the years so that no-one seemed to notice the fact that he was actually a year *older* than Jessie Royce Landis who played his mother in the film. Lehman's script was not only witty but also very sexy – in fact, too sexy for the American censor when it came to the final lovey-dovey shot of Grant and Saint in their Pullman berth. The censor, Geoffrey Shurlock, memo-ed Hitchcock that that there should be a line inserted referring to 'Mrs Thornhill' for greater propriety. That done, another shot, of a train going into a tunnel, was then also added belatedly, not to say mischievously, by Hitchcock to end the film. Writes Bill Krohn in *Hitchcock at Work*: 'Noisily sanctioned by marriage, thanks to Mr Shurlock, and barely obscured by the veil of metaphor, the last shot of *North by Northwest* is the most explicit depiction of the bottom-line facts of the sexual act ever pulled off under the Production Code, and a vengeance worthy of the Master.'[156]

One of Hitchcock's most expensive films (budgeted at over $3.1 million, it ended up costing more than $4.2 million) as well as his longest (at 136 minutes), it was also one of the most successful critically – hailed as a return to peerless comedy-thriller form – and commercially. Awards-wise, though, it had the misfortune to coincide with *Ben-Hur*, which practically effected a clean sweep in 1959. A year earlier he had received a Golden Globe for his television series, which also, in the wake of yet another Oscar snub for *North by Northwest*, earned him an Emmy nomination for his 'individual direction' of the *Lamb to the Slaughter* episode from the third season of *Alfred Hitchcock Presents*. However, the degree of control he could exert over his small-screen career didn't necessarily extend to either the films or to his personal life. In 1958, a year after he'd had an emergency gallbladder and gallstones operation, Hitchcock was shocked to discover that Alma had been diagnosed with cervical cancer and required immediate life-saving surgery. On a much happier note, the couple enjoyed the company of two granddaughters, Mary and Teresa. A third, Kathleen, arrived in 1959. Their mother, Pat, still dabbled in acting occasionally, with appearances in several episodes of the TV series and, of course, a telling cameo still to come in her father's next, and arguably most celebrated, film.

What Hitchcock had wanted to direct next was the London-set story of an amnesiac judge accused of killing a prostitute. Adapted by Samuel Taylor from the novel, *No Bail for the Judge* by Henry Cecil (whose witty legal comedy *Brothers in Law* was filmed in the mid 1950s by the Boultings), the project was to co-star old Hitchcock hand John Williams, Audrey Hepburn, as the judge's investigative daughter, and Laurence Harvey. After extensive pre-production including much on-site research about the London underworld, the film suddenly foundered. Hepburn, so enthusiastic at first, decided to pass for various reasons, not least due to the fact she suffered a miscarriage. While she was convalescing, noted her biographer Alexander Walker, 'Audrey took her first comprehensive look at the complete script … In her present state, having just lost a child, she reacted with disbelieving horror. Her character was going to be raped in a London park; even in her usual good health, she would have found the scene repugnant.'[157] Hitchcock was, however, determined to hold her to her contract especially when her latest film, *The Nun's Story*, proved a big hit.

'I beg permission to mention by name only four people who have given me the most affection, appreciation and encouragement, and constant collaboration. The first of the four is a film editor, the second is a script writer, the third is the mother of my daughter, Pat, and the fourth is as fine a cook as ever performed miracles in a domestic kitchen, and their names are Alma Reville.'

ALFRED HITCHCOCK dedicating his Lifetime Achievement Award from the American Film Institute in 1979

Vera Miles, John Gavin and Janet Leigh in a publicity still taken for the promotion of **Psycho**

Hepburn offered the best, non-legal, riposte: she became pregnant again, which meant that the film would have to be put on hold once more. The director knew when he was beaten, although he apparently forever held it against the elfin actress.

So he turned instead to a project whose hue, scale and subject matter could not have contrasted more with his previous glossy VistaVision thrillers. If TV had taught him one thing, it was speed and spareness of production and he wanted to shoot

Psycho fast and no-frills, he said at the time, the way he would an episode of his series. Robert Bloch's eponymous novel, loosely based on the Wisconsin cannibal-killer Ed Gein, was worked on first by one of Hitchcock's regular television writers, James Cavanagh. Then the director, who thought his draft unusable, turned to Joseph Stefano to tease out the terrifying tale of a on-a-whim thief Marion Crane, boyfriend Sam, her sister Lila and a private eye called Arbogast who all enter the strange world of mother-fixated motel owner Norman Bates. Although Bloch's pulpy novel is quite faithfully followed, Stefano came up with the idea of making Marion the main focus of the first half of the film with Bates moving centre stage in the second. He also told Hitchcock, "'I'd like to see Marion shacking up with Sam on her lunch hour". The moment I said "shack up" or anything like that, Hitchcock, being a very salacious man, adored it. I said, "We'll find out what the girl is all about, see her steal the money and head for Sam – on the way this horrendous thing happens to her." He thought it was spectacular. I think that idea got me the job.' [158] What Stefano didn't like at all was the character of Bates as originally written by Bloch: a drunken homicidal fortysome-thing who peeps through holes. How would he feel, Hitchcock asked him, if he was played by the gangly good-looking 27-year-old Anthony Perkins. Stefano told him, "'Now you're talking." I suddenly saw a tender young man you could feel incredibly sorry for. I could really rope in an audience with someone like him.'[159] The 'horrendous thing' that happens to Marion is, of course, her murder in the shower which was the one element of the novel that most appealed to Hitchcock, especially its suddenness. Minute planning of that particular scene and the novelty of making the murder seem even more unexpected by the early killing-off of the film's nominal star, Janet Leigh, were clearly irresistible.

The casting of Anthony Perkins as the 'psycho' Norman Bates in Psycho *was a stroke of genius by Hitchcock. The actor was never able to lose the shadow of this role in his later career*

When Hitchcock told Paramount about *Psycho*, the studio was not impressed. It tried to deter him first by imposing a low budget and then told him that all the sound stages at Paramount were booked. Undaunted, Hitchcock accepted the $800,000 budget, deferring his own salary in return for owning 60 per cent of the negative, organised a 30-day shooting schedule, moved production to the Revue Studios on the Universal lot where he was already shooting his TV series, and instructed cinematographer John L Russell, a veteran of *Alfred Hitchcock Presents*, to film in black and white (*Psycho* would, of course, be unthinkable in colour – yet another strike against the pointless shot-for-shot remake in 1998). As was standard practice for TV but not features, Hitchcock planned regular use of two cameras, and production reports would note the rental of sometimes three or even four cameras a day. His cast was inexpensive too; for instance, Perkins, who already owed Paramount a film under an old contract, was snared for just $40,000.

Filming began on 11 November 1959 and a month later, they were shooting *Psycho*'s most famous sequence, the killing of Marion Crane (or 'Mary', as she was first called in Stefano's extremely graphic script) in the motel shower. Hitchcock invited Saul Bass, who'd designed the vivid title sequences for *Vertigo* and *North by Northwest* (and would also do so for *Psycho*), to create a storyboard for the shower killing, and he responded with 48 drawings, which certainly provided the basis for the terrifying series of monochrome images that resulted. 'It took us seven days to shoot that scene, and there were 70 camera setups for 45 seconds of footage,' Hitchcock told Truffaut.[161] Beginning with a close-up shot of Norman's eye pressed to a peephole and ending on Marion's dead, staring eye, the scene, like the whole film, is genius as much for what it doesn't show as for the more obvious moments of grandstanding *grand guignol*. Bass' contribution – if perhaps not quite as great as the man himself apparently claimed when suggesting he'd actually co-directed the shower scene with Hitchcock – along with Bernard Herrmann's is inestimable. Hitchcock had originally designated the shower scene as music-less. The composer responded with high-pitched violins

'He [Hitchcock] was so painstakingly interested in what I had to say and was so eager to accept ideas of all kinds to the point when I would sometimes come into his dressing room in the morning with the re-written pages and I would offer these to him, and he would turn away from the London Times *and say, "Are they any good?" I'd say, "I don't know, shouldn't we be saving time if you would go over them now." He'd say, "I'm sure they'll be very good." I said, "Don't you want to see them now?" He replied, "Enchant me later!"'[160]*

ANTHONY PERKINS
on the filming of *Psycho*

that shredded already tattered nerves. The director admitted that the soundtrack enhanced the scene but was actually even prouder of the fact he managed to get away with the sight and sound of a lavatory flushing, something then unprecedented under the Production Code.

The killing of Arbogast (Martin Balsam) at the top of the stairs in the old dark house was, if not as iconic, no less dazzling as we see the private eye, face bloodied, toppling backwards after a sudden attack, filmed from above, by the transvestite Norman. First the staircase and the room behind it were shot. Then the actor was placed in a chair on a 'dolly' going down the stairs. The chair was lowered at the speed of a stabbed man falling backwards. The second piece of film was printed on the first without any obvious loss of startling effect. The famous gothic-looking *Psycho* house, which would later become a popular feature of the Universal Studios Tour (although its location was different during actual filming), proved yet another of the film's iconic images. Up on a hill above the Bates Motel, it oozed menace. Did its startling 'look' emanate from the imagination of the set designers or perhaps even the film's 'pictorial consultant' Saul Bass? Most likely is that Hitchcock himself – an art buff of some repute whose collection included works by Rodin, Klee and Odilon Redon – may have influenced it from his extensive knowledge of modern painting. It seems no coincidence – and the claim was recently underlined in a new book about the American artist Edward Hopper by Ivo Franzfelder – that the building was inspired by a 1925 canvas, *House by the Railroad*. The resemblance is uncanny.

The amount of control Hitchcock exerted over the shooting of *Psycho* was extended to the marketing when he insisted on advertising stressing that 'no-one will be allowed to enter the cinema after the film has started'. He also, rather bravely, insisted that the critics see the film with the general public, risking a potential backlash from fussy scribes. He'd have been delighted with *Variety* which described 'Hitchcock up to his clavicle in whimsicality … He's gotten in gore, in the form of a couple of graphically depicted knife murders, a story that's far out in Freudian motivations, and now and then injects little amusing plot items that suggest the whole thing is not to be taken seriously.' Others didn't get the joke. Apparently *The Observer*'s C A Lejeune walked out after the shower scene in disgust and retired from film-reviewing not long after that. The public flocked to the film, more, one suspects, for therapeutic scares than tongue-in-cheek laughs, making it Hitchcock's most successful ever. According to John Russell Taylor, it grossed some $15 million on its first release in the States of which Hitchcock's share was $2.5 million presented to him by Paramount and 'by far and away the largest amount they had ever paid an independent producer'.[163]

This gold strike didn't, however, follow Hitchcock to the Academy Awards a year later where he was unsuccessful for the fifth, and last, time in the Best Director stakes, losing out eventually to Billy Wilder who won his third Oscar in that category for *The Apartment*. Some consolation for Hitchcock seemed to come from an unlikely quarter as he declared 'I have brought murder back into the home where it belongs.'

Chapter 12

The Great Inventor

After *Psycho*, his sixth and last film for Paramount, Hitchcock began a contractual tie-up with Universal, which would remain intact until the end of his life. His deal, concluded with the studio early in 1962, also coincided with the final stage in the take-over of the 50-year-old film company by Lew Wasserman and MCA, a complex move that had been initiated in 1959. He already knew the place well from the production of *Psycho* and his ongoing television series, and also had in Wasserman, who'd had to forego his agency business to become perhaps the most powerful Hollywood mogul of his time, a friend in the highest place. Hitchcock's bungalow on the lot would become a veritable home-from-home. Some years later, the writer David Freeman who collaborated with Hitchcock on *Short Night*, an abortive project based on the escape of convicted spy George Blake, recalled the director's new digs: 'The office is standard Universal issue. Sort of pseudo English-manor-house. To call it a bungalow is to understate the case a bit. It's a bungalow the way summer houses in Newport are cottages. This bungalow has two levels, a screening room, a dining room, many offices, an art department

and cutting rooms.'[164] Hitchcock was still, just, in his old office at Paramount when another writer, Evan Hunter, aka Ed McBain, was summoned to the presence to discuss a film adaptation of Daphne du Maurier's short story, *The Birds*. Hunter, a successful novelist in his own right, had already written one teleplay as well as having had two of his short stories adapted for the TV series so there was 'history'. Du Maurier's story, first published in a 1952 anthology, was the dialogue-less tale of a Cornish farmer and his wife whose cottage is inexplicably invaded by birds. Hunter's

Rod Taylor and Tippi Hedren took the lead roles in Hitchcock's ambitious thriller based on Daphne du Maurier's novella **The Birds**

brief was 'to forget the story entirely.'[165] Hitchcock was not interested in either the British characters or, less still, the West Country location. It was all about the title and, with the director's interest further fuelled after reading various shock-horror news reports about the phenomenon, the idea of birds attacking human beings.

In fact, Hitchcock was seriously juggling two projects – a third, if you also count his notion of a suspense thriller set in Disneyland – at the time. He'd just been introduced to Winston Graham's newly-published novel, *Marnie*, and saw possibilities in this contemporary female-narrated story of sexual intrigue from another British writer much better known for his historical *Poldark* series. *Marnie* especially interested him because he saw in it the chance to 'discover' a new 'cool Hitchcock blonde' that he'd be able to mould from the outset. He and Alma found her in 30-year-old Minnesota-born model Nathalie 'Tippi' Hedren during a diet drink commercial while they were watching daytime television. Soon Hedren, mother of a four-year-old daughter (later actress Melanie Griffith), was being groomed intensively for future stardom. Meanwhile, Hunter was happily beavering away on his assignment with Grace Kelly and Cary Grant firmly in mind as the couple who after meeting 'cute' in a bird store in San Francisco are gradually drawn into an unfolding tale of avian horror 50 miles up the coast in Bodega Bay, a quiet seaside town. 'It was,' wrote Hunter, 'on one of my solitary strolls that the idea came to me. I take full credit – or blame, as the case may be – for what I suggested to Hitch … "a screwball comedy that turns into stark terror".'[166] The idea clearly appealed to the director – for the time being anyway. Hunter admitted that Hitchcock should probably have junked his idea then and there but 'instead we marched ahead confidently, blithely trying to graft upon du

Maurier's simple tale of apocalyptic terror a slick story about two improbable lovers confronted with an even more improbable situation – birds attacking humans.'[167]

There would also be no Kelly and Grant but instead, Hitchcock's inexperienced new protégée Hedren as feckless socialite Melanie Daniels, and rugged Australian actor Rod Taylor, as thirtysomething lawyer Mitch Brenner, who stills lives at home with his possessive mother (Jessica Tandy). Hitchcock's typically meticulous pre-planning, much of it centred around the birds themselves, couldn't however have prepared him for what he told Truffaut was a first in his long film-making experience: losing faith in the script after he'd started shooting. So, he claims, he started to improvise here and there, changing stuff and making up things on the spur because either they seemed 'old fashioned' or else made no 'sense' as written. He also, Hunter said, got in touch with an old friend, the English writer V S Pritchett, inviting him first to comment on the script in two of its re-writes and then later to add a scene. In fact, Hunter speculated, Pritchett was probably responsible for the film's very unHollywoodlike ending as opposed to his much more upbeat (but rejected) finale in which Melanie, Mitch and his mother speed away towards a beautiful, unfeathery sunrise.

Yet, for a film which might have defined the expression 'high concept' that would become common currency in Hollywood 30 years later, characters and exposition seemed hardly to matter so long as he got the horror bits right. After an as-audience-pleasing shocker as *Psycho*, the expectation was rampant. As well as regular collaborators like production designer Robert Boyle, editor George Tomasini, composer Herrmann (here designated 'sound consultant' for his eerily music-less accompaniment), and cinematographer Burks, Hitchcock added three more key human

161

components to the avian equation. British-born matte artist and painter Albert Whitlock, who'd had worked years earlier as a teenager for Hitchcock on *The Man Who Knew Too Much* before heading to Hollywood where he eventually became an Oscar-winning visual effects wizard, was 'pictorial consultant'; Ray Berwick, the bird trainer; Harold Michaelson, illustrator; and veteran animator/effects technician Ub Iwerks, like Whitlock an alumnus of Disney, was 'special photographic designer', who oversaw the entire effects package.

Boyle said that when he did some of his design sketches for the film he had Edvard Munch's painting 'The Scream' in mind, as 'to me [it] was a symbol of the terror that birds can strike in the heart of many people'.[168] Michaelson drew vivid storyboards for scenes involving the birds themselves. Among Whitlock's many brilliant matte paintings was the literal 'bird's eye view' of Bodega Bay which was combined with a petrol station fire filmed on a parking lot at Universal. Now all Whitlock had to do was create the impression of birds descending from behind the camera into the fiery chaos – 'I had heard that there were birds nesting in the 350-foot cliffs at Santa Cruz Islands. It occurred to me that if a cameraman were to get above this cliff and throw fish –charm them out of the cliffs – the birds would dive for the fish, which is exactly what happened. Then we "rotoscoped" [a form of anima-tion] them off the film and put them over the painting. It took three months to do.'[169] Berwick's expertise – following Hitchcock's decision to dump the idea of using mechanical birds for, as much as possible, the real thing – was experienced often painfully by Hedren when it took seven days to film (for one minute of screen time) her shocking close encounter with gulls, crows and ravens in the climactic attic scene. Hitchcock confined her to a cagelike room and then had crew members throw hundreds of live birds

at her while others were tied by nylon threads to her arms and legs. After being pecked on the eyelid, the actress became hysterical and filming finally had to be suspended, but not before the director – persistent or simply sadistic? – had achieved plenty of extraordinary footage. As Hitchcock's own marketing slogan for the film put it, '*The Birds* is coming!'

While *The Birds* was still filming, Hitchcock announced to the world that Grace Kelly would return from her royal retirement in Monaco to play the title role in his next film, *Marnie*. Whether it was the lack of protocol or the disturbing possibility that Her Serene Highness would be required to play a sexually frigid, compulsive thief with a fear of the colour red who's raped therapeutically on her wedding night by her new husband, the Riviera connection was never consummated. So Hitchcock turned instead to his in-house star Hedren, who after her experiences on *The Birds* and her growing concerns about the overly attentive director, visibly cooled on her mentor during filming. And vice-versa, so that after one particular shouting match in which she apparently made some rude reference to his height, he'd only speak to her through a third party. Before they even got to actual production, the script had been through the grinder, starting with Joseph Stefano before moving on to Evan Hunter for his second bite of Hitchcock. The experience was reasonably short-lived. Hunter had made it clear that he felt the rape scene as described to him by the director would work against the film, with loss of audience sympathy for his male lead. 'Hitch,' recalled Hunter, 'held up his hands the way directors do when they're framing a shot. Palms out, fingers together, thumbs extended and touching to form a perfect square. Moving his hands towards my face, like a camera coming in for a close shot, he said, "Evan, when he sticks it in her, I want that camera right on her *face*!" Many years later, when I told Jay Presson Allen [who had eventual screen credit] how much his description of that scene has bothered me, she said, "You just got bothered by the scene that was his reason for making the movie. You just wrote your ticket back to New York."' [171]

In his first flush of Bond-age when selected to play Marnie's husband, Sean Connery did as well as he could with a role which even the director, who apparently admired the actor's performance, later admitted, a little discourteously, probably needed an older man not to mention 'a real gentleman, a more elegant man than we had'.[172] Hedren, despite her travails on both *The Birds* and *Marnie* and contrary to some of the contemporary critical carping about her skill and inexperience, is, with considerable hindsight, oddly affecting in both roles. There's almost an otherworldly, an if you like lack-of-knowing, quality about her performances which seems to work well for both Melanie and Marnie, a pair of fragile anti-heroines. Neither the very expensive *The Birds* nor *Marnie*, which, at $2 million, cost half the first film, set the box office alight – the first made a small profit, the second a tiny loss – as Hitchcock switched his thoughts, in the mid 1960s, from horror and psycho-drama to the Cold War.

Hitchcock had made 23 films in the first two decades after arriving in Hollywood; he officially made just eight in 20 years after that. In fact, that total should actually read nine if you count, as no official lists do, a sadly-neglected addition to his filmography called *The Westcliff Cine Club Visits Mr Hitchcock*. This 16-minute gem came about as the result of a letter to Hitchcock early in 1963 from the Westcliff Cine and 35mm Club in his native Essex inviting him to become a patron. Would Mr Hitchcock confirm by letter or perhaps even via an audio tape if he'd be prepared to accept. Hitchcock's office in Hollywood quickly replied querying, to the club's great surprise, if a film would be preferred. The club's founder president, John Kennedy Melling, warned his PR man John Wright – who'd written the original letter to Hitchcock – that there might be a catch. So Wright, perhaps more in hope than any genuine expectation, then asked boldly for a 35mm colour contribution. It arrived within two

Tippi Hedren in **Marnie**, *her second leading role for Hitchcock*

weeks. This rarely-seen collector's item starts with a car drawing up at the entrance to Universal Studios where the gatekeeper acknowledges the arrival of 'the Westcliff Cine Club' before directing it on to the lot where he says Mr Hitchcock is waiting at Stage 18. The film then cuts to the director himself talking enthusiastically and, on occasion, very wittily, direct to camera about some long-ago memories of Essex, notably the London-Tilbury & Southend Railway and of 'dreary' days on the Thames. After a brief guided tour of the studio, Hitchcock expounds on some of his more favoured theories of filmmaking, notably the 'language' of editing, before ending on a plea that audiences flock to his next film, *The Birds*, because he needs 'to feed his starving wife and child'. The film was premiered in June that year at the Kursaal Estuary Suite in Southend-on-Sea, Westcliff's more famous neighbour.

Age – he was heading towards 70 – and fashion, especially at a time when the notion of the 'Swinging Sixties' and youth-at-all-costs started to infect the creative arts worldwide, would make 'the money' warier than ever. Among the still, even vaguely, active A-list of Hollywood survivors from the Victorian era – like John Ford, Howard Hawks, Frank Capra and Henry Hathaway – Hitchcock would go on longer than most – though not quite as long as another 1899 baby, George Cukor, who was still directing after Hitchcock died. But the gaps in between were getting bigger than ever. For a director who liked to surround himself with familiar faces in the workplace, time and circumstance was also taking its toll. George Tomasini, who had cut nine films for Hitchcock starting with *Rear Window*, died in 1964, and three years later the faithful Robert Burks, together with his wife, perished tragically in a fire at his home.

His relationship with Bernard Herrmann, whose collaborative work had done as much as anyone, if not more than most, to establish the director's unique 'brand', finally broke down altogether during Hitchcock's 50th production. As so often before, he'd been delving into the past for future inspiration and among the projects he toyed with briefly were Buchan's novel *The Three Hostages*, J M Barrie's play *Mary Rose* – as a specific 'vehicle' for the contracted Hedren – and the curiously titled *R.R.R.R.*, about the day-to-day running of a big hotel. He had also conjured up his own memories of the headline-grabbing defection to the Soviet Union many years earlier of the British spies, Burgess and Maclean. Hitchcock's fascination with the subject matter lay with the idea of trying to view the scandal from, as he told Truffaut, Mrs Maclean's point of view. In other words, betrayal on a domestic and international scale. Despite Hitchcock's own assertion, there appears to be, if you believe certain sources, some slight confusion at this point over the project's motivation. Donald Spoto, for instance, suggests that Hitchcock's interest appeared to lie rather with the reaction of Mary Burgess, the wife of the openly gay half of the fleeing pair which would add an extra layer to the intrigue. What, however, eventually became *Torn Curtain* proved to be rather a long way away from those facts, although the tiniest germ remained. It was, however, a sign of the changing times that the studio insisted on the stars Hitchcock *must* have in the film: Paul Newman and Julie Andrews.

Hitchcock had first gone to the Irish novelist Brian Moore for a screenplay and when he wasn't satisfied with that, turned to the prolific writing team of Keith Waterhouse and Willis Hall for what turned out to be – after yet another arbitration with the Writers Guild – an uncredited revise. In box office terms, Newman and Andrews, fresh from her *Mary Poppins* and *Sound of Music* triumphs, could not have been 'hotter'. For Hitchcock, the idea of having stars who'd eat up more than 20 per cent of his $5 million budget was already anathema. To have those particular stars with their particular baggage meant also the nature of the story would have to change drastically and dramatically. And he was, after all, *the* name-above-the-title. But if he wanted Universal's money, he would simply have to accept Newman and

Andrews as the unlikely couple. They were, by now, no longer even remotely Mr and Mrs Maclean (less still Mr and Mrs Burgess) of London, England but instead the impossibly good-looking American nuclear physicist Professor Michael Armstrong and his well-scrubbed fiancée/assistant Sarah Sherman of mid-Atlantic origin. Naturally, the square-jawed academic wasn't really planning to defect but actually working as a double agent – unbeknownst to his girlfriend – in order to wheedle a crucial formula out of a top Soviet scientist.

In between signing for the film and start of shooting, Newman was particularly exercised that the eventual script had significantly changed in character from the one outlined by Hitchcock in their original meeting. According to Daniel O'Brien, one of the actor's biographers, 'covering fourteen main points, Newman's detailed critique included the overall tone, specific scenes and his own character. Many elements lacked credibility, undercutting the suspense. Newman also disliked the title – "a trifle arch"'.[173] Actor and director, ever suspicious of the 'Method' school, also had their moments during filming. When, before one scene, Newman asked Hitchcock about his 'motivation', the director famously replied, 'Your motivation, Mr Newman, is your salary.'[174]

As had happened on so many other occasions, Hitchcock seemed to be less interested in the big picture than in just one particularly showy sequence. This was specifically designed to demonstrate how very difficult and very painful it can be, and especially how long it can take, to kill a man – in this case, Newman's sinister, leather-jacketed, gum-chewing 'minder' Gromek (Wolfgang Kieling), who having discovered the Prof's little secret confronts him and a farmer's wife in a remote country farmhouse. Wrote William Schoell in *Stay Out of the Shower*: 'As Gromek uses the phone to call the authorities, Newman rips it off the wall. He can't use Gromek's gun to shoot him, because it will alert his associates waiting outside. The woman tries to stab Gromek but the blade of the knife snaps off. As Newman and Gromek grapple, she grabs a shovel and begins to bash him on the legs. Finally they have Gromek on his knees and slowly drag him over to the oven, where they both hold his head in as the gas does its work. Newman's face mirrors both relief and disgust at what he's had to do. The whole sequence is breathlessly edited, beginning with extreme close-ups of Gromek's finger-stabbing as they talk before the murder.'[175] Would that deliciously macabre scene, far and away the most memorable in a mostly forgettable Cold War potboiler, have been even more memorable with Bernard Herrmann's fully orchestral score? Cinema audiences never got a chance to find out because Hitchcock, perhaps mindful of the studio's desire for more obviously marketable music – a song and a soundtrack album, no less – objected forcefully to the composer's more traditional stylings, thus sadly

ending their long and potent collaboration. John Addison, who had won the Oscar for his lively *Tom Jones* score, wrote a lighter accompaniment but the murder sequence itself would remain unaccompanied – perhaps in silent homage to Herrmann? – in the release version of the film, noticeable, remarked *Variety*, for 'its lack of zip and pacing.' Apart from the plodding script, there was, as even Hitchcock would note, a distinct lack of chemistry between the stars Universal had foisted on the director,

Hitchcock pointing out
directions on the set of Topaz

171

with Newman's intensity contrasting uneasily with Andrews' blandness.

Hitchcock couldn't even plead the excuse of unwanted star power for the even more disappointing second half of his Cold War 'double'. Indeed it's difficult to think what, if anything – apart from the chance to keep working on the eve of his 70th birthday – attracted him to *Topaz*, arguably the lowest point in his long directing career. Based on Leon Uris's novel, it was a thinly disguised if convoluted reworking of a real-life Franco-Russian spy scandal set against the background of the 1962 Cuban Missile Crisis. The rights were already owned by Universal and Hitchcock seemed almost pathetically grateful to be able to latch on to this in-house assignment for the chance to get back behind the camera. He'd reached that stage of his career where in between trying to develop new projects, his public life seemed mainly to consist of a series of lifetime achievement awards, international honours and festival homages. At the 40th Academy Awards in April 1968, which were postponed for 48 hours because of the assassination of Dr Martin Luther King, he stepped on to the stage at the Santa Monica Civic Auditorium to receive the Irving G Thalberg Memorial Award for 'consistent high quality of production' throughout his career. On a night one of his former stars, Gregory Peck, also received an honorary award, the audience must have thought it could be in for a typically witty and perhaps even slightly mischievous speech from the veteran filmmaker. In the event, he simply said 'Thank you' and walked off. The overriding feeling that this was some kind of consolation prize for all his earlier Oscar disappointments wasn't lost on the audience, commentators and, of course, Hitchcock himself.

For *Topaz*, Uris himself wrote a script, which the director considered unusable so he summoned his old friend Samuel

Taylor to do a last-minute rewrite. Not even last-minute surgery would have saved this unwieldy production, a kind of international equivalent of the hybrid film species still known as a 'Euro-pudding'. While there were no such distractions as Hollywood stars, there was instead the obvious ill-ease of a no-name cast sounding as if they were performing English in a foreign language. The likes of Frederick Stafford (real name Friedrich

173

Strobel von Stein), Karin Dor and Per Axel Arosenius strained an already ropy script in a veritable Babel of accents. The locations were equally international but, like the cast, mostly uninteresting, including Denmark, France and New York, as well as the back lot at Universal doubling for Cuba since the island itself was clearly a no-go area. Hitchcock tried to surround himself with as much familiarity as possible behind the camera. As well as regulars like Edith Head, Henry Bumstead, Albert Whitlock and Herbert Coleman, there were other significant returnees such as British cinematographer Jack Hildyard, who'd last worked with the director on *Jamaica Inn*, and the actor John Forsythe, for the first time since *The Trouble with Harry*. It's difficult to recall even one classic Hitchcock 'moment' in a mostly anonymous film, which he seems to have directed by numbers rather than from even a handful of inspired storyboards. While *Torn Curtain* had at least managed to turn a tiny profit, *Topaz*, deservedly scorned by most critics, was a box-office disaster, probably the worst of his career since going to Hollywood.

And still the honours kept pouring in. There was the Directors Guild of America (DGA) Lifetime Achievement Award which, following eight unsuccessful DGA nominations for Best Director, rather echoed his belated honorary Oscar. The Los Angeles County Museum of Art and the Lincoln Center in New York accorded him Gala Tributes. Away from his adopted home, Hitchcock had long been a darling of French critics-turned-filmmakers like Rohmer, Chabrol and, especially, Truffaut (who poured his infectious admiration into one of the most quoted-ever books on the director first published in 1966 under the title *Le Cinema selon Hitchcock*). As if to formalise this Gallic *estime*, he received from the French government the title of Officier des Arts et des Lettres in 1969 followed, two years later, by the award of Chevalier de la Légion d'honneur. From Britain came the honour of the Society of Film and Television Arts' (later BAFTA) first Fellowship. Meanwhile, still overly fond of wine and food – as both a gourmet and gourmand – his weight continued to fluctuate between mighty and massive. His and the still birdlike Alma's, health also wavered – sometimes dramatically – as they combined an almost dully conventional home life with regular trips abroad for fun and publicity purposes.

But despite the acclaim and the untold riches, work remained all-important. Back in England, he directed *Frenzy* (see Chapter 1) which for all the reservations about its often curious content eventually proved a very welcome return to box-office form for the director. It had also been another, longer, opportunity to revisit the old country which he'd done in only very short bursts since making *Stage Fright*, mainly for publicity purposes. On one of these occasions, in 1969, some months before the release of *Topaz*, he'd been interviewed by fellow filmmaker Bryan Forbes on the stage of the National Film Theatre as part of the John Player Lecture series. Forbes, who'd also just become head of production at Hitchcock's alma mater, Elstree Studios, presided over a memorable occasion which provided a forum for Hitchcock's wit, much insight, a little self-deprecation and just the odd flash of annoyance. Forbes recalled: 'I didn't like him. During the entire hour-long interview, he didn't actually give any recognition that I might be a colleague. He treated me in a rather cursory way. At one point, I said to him, "It was a great pity that you, a master of a genre, and Graham Greene, the master of his, never worked together". He replied: "I've never read Graham Greene." I then said, "I doubt that's true and if it is, I think the remark is beneath you." He didn't care for that.'[176] Hitchcock's response may, of course, have been to do with the fact that of all the critics

'There is great confusion between the words "mystery" and "suspense". The two things are absolutely miles apart. Mystery is an intellectual process like in a "whodunit". But suspense is essentially an emotional process. You can only get the suspense element going by giving the audience information … the mystery form has no particular appeal to me, because it is merely a fact of mystifying an audience, which I don't think is enough.'

HITCHCOCK addressing the AFI's Center for Advanced Studies in 1970

in the director's British years, Greene perhaps gave him the hardest time, and the memory had lingered. But there were many lighter moments during the packed event. Asked about *Marnie* and whether the ship we see looking distorted in one scene is 'presumably symptomatic of her tortured childhood?', Hitchcock replied, 'No, we had a lousy scene painter.' And to the query, 'Mr Hitchcock, you seem to have a nice sense of humour which you obviously had before you established yourself directing thrillers. How come you've never made comedies?', he replied, to thunderous applause, 'But every film I make is a comedy!'

His 53rd and last film – though almost until the day of his death nearly four years later he still entertained plans of making more movies, notably the *Short Night* project – was *Family Plot*. With working titles of *One Plus One Equals One* and *Deception*, the source material was Victor Canning's 1972 thriller *The Rainbird Pattern*, transplanted by screenwriter Ernest Lehman from its very English roots to a thoroughly American milieu for a comedy-drama of kidnap and psychic scams. As with *Torn Curtain*, Universal put pressure on Hitchcock for a big-name cast but as he'd just helped replenish their coffers with good unstarry actors on *Frenzy*, he got his own way, signing up Bruce Dern, Barbara Harris, Karen Black, 86-year-old Cathleen Nesbitt – whom he would have relished on the London stage after the Great War – and Roy Thinnes. The hapless Thinnes, playing the villain of the piece, lasted just a month of shooting before he was replaced by the more obviously nefarious William Devane, he of the shark-toothed smile. George Perry, journalist and author of *The Films of Alfred Hitchcock*, was on the set of *Family Plot*. 'I was,' he recalled, 'actually there on the day it wrapped. I'd like to say it was the last time he shot anything, but I think he did one or two experimental things later. As we know, he harboured the wish to make other

films [like *The Short Night*] after *Family Plot* and worked on ideas. The prospect probably kept him alive as it did for other directors whose day was done, such as Billy Wilder.'

Minor Hitchcock by the standards of his best films, it was, however, still considerably better scripted, more suspenseful and wittier than some of the other, and costlier, works in the last decade or so of his working life. Roger Ebert wrote of *Family Plot* in the *Chicago Sun-Times*: 'It's a delight for two contradictory reasons: because it's pure Hitchcock, with its meticulous construction and attention to detail, and because it's something new for Hitchcock – a macabre comedy, essentially. He doesn't go for shock here, or for violent effects, but for the gradual tightening of a narrative noose.' If he had to bow out on one film, how better this one than, say, *Topaz*.

During the final 12 months of his life, either side of his 80th birthday in August 1979, there were two more important accolades. In March 1979 he was the seventh recipient of the American Film Institute's Life Achievement Award, following John Ford, James Cagney, Orson Welles, William Wyler, Bette Davis and Henry Fonda. To date, he and David Lean, in 1990, remain the only native-born Britons on the prestigious list. Finally, in the 1980 New Year's Honours List, Hitchcock was named an honorary Knight Commander of the British Empire for his services to British culture. Four months later, on 29 April, he died peacefully at his home in Bellagio Road. Hitchcock, wrote Eric Rohmer and Claude Chabrol in their eponymous 1957 book on the director, was 'one of the greatest inventors of form in the history of the cinema. Perhaps the only directors who can be compared with him in this respect are Murnau and Eisenstein … Here, form does not merely embellish content, but actually creates it.' Hitchcock's own preferred epitaph would have been, 'This is what we do to bad little boys.' It finally read: 'I'm in on a plot.'

Notes

Chapter 1 interviews with Colin Brewer, Jon Finch, Peter Handford, Alec McCowen, Gil Taylor and Paul Wilson by the author during 2004/5

1. François Truffaut, *Hitchcock* (Secker & Warburg, London: 1968) p 24.
2. Truffaut, *Hitchcock*, p 24.
3. Truffaut, *Hitchcock*, p 22.
4. John Russell Taylor, *Hitch: The Life & Times of Alfred Hitchcock* (Berkley, New York: 1980) p 9.
5. Donald Spoto, *The Dark Side of Genius: The Life of Alfred Hitchcock* (Plexus, London: 1994) p 33.
6. Russell Taylor, *Hitch*, p 15.
7. Russell Taylor, *Hitch*, p 19.
8. Spoto, *The Dark Side of Genius*, p 42.
9. Russell Taylor, *Hitch*, p 15.
10. Sidney Gottlieb (ed), *Hitchcock on Hitchcock* (Faber and Faber, London: 1997) p 10.
11. Russell Taylor, *Hitch*, p 40.
12. Patrick McGilligan, *Fritz Lang* (Faber and Faber, London: 1997) p 122.

13. Russell Taylor, *Hitch*, p 55.
14. Truffaut, *Hitchcock*, p 38.
15. Truffaut, *Hitchcock*, p 38.
16. Truffaut, *Hitchcock*, p 42.
17. Matthew Sweet, *Shepperton Babylon* (Faber and Faber, London: 2005) p 62.
18. Truffaut, *Hitchcock*, p 45.
19. Howard Maxford, *The A-Z of Hitchcock* (BT Batsford, London: 2002) p 217.
20. Michael Powell, *A Life in Movies* (Faber and Faber, London: 2000) p 186.
21. Russell Taylor, *Hitch*, p 87.
22. Russell Taylor, *Hitch*, p 82 (from National Film Archive).
23. Paul Condon and Jim Sangster, *The Complete Hitchcock* (Virgin, London: 1999) pp 24–5.
24. Gottlieb (ed), *Hitchcock on Hitchcock*, p 254.
25. Truffaut, *Hitchcock*, p 67.
26. Truffaut, *Hitchcock*, p 62.
27. Bryan Langley BSC, interview with the author (10 June 2005).
28. Langley interview.
29. Langley interview.
30. Truffaut, *Hitchcock*, p 67.
31. Truffaut, *Hitchcock*, p 68.
32. Spoto, *The Dark Side of Genius*, p 141.
33. Truffaut, *Hitchcock*, p 73.
34. Spoto, *The Dark Side of Genius*, p 143.
35. Truffaut, *Hitchcock*, p 74.
36. Spoto, *The Dark Side of Genius*, p 143.
37. Truffaut, *Hitchcock*, p 75.
38. Sweet, *Shepperton Babylon*, p 169.

39. Truffaut, *Hitchcock*, p 77.

40. Spoto, *The Dark Side of Genius*, p 152.

41. Spoto, *The Dark Side of Genius*, p 152.

42. Spoto, *The Dark Side of Genius*, p 153.

43. Gottlieb (ed), *Hitchcock on Hitchcock*, p 24.

44. Gottlieb (ed), *Hitchcock on Hitchcock*, p 24.

45. Truffaut, *Hitchcock*, p 87.

46. Gottlieb (ed), *Hitchcock on Hitchcock*, p 186.

47. Rudy Behlmar (ed), *Memo from David O Selznick* (The Viking Press, New York: 1972) p 251.

48. Hilton Tims, *Once a Wicked Lady* (Virgin Books, London: 1989) p 75.

49. Roy Ward Baker, *The Director's Cut* (Reynolds & Hearn, London: 2000), pp 31–2.

50. Ward Baker, *The Director's Cut*, p 31.

51. Russell Taylor, *Hitch*, p 139.

52. Russell Taylor, *Hitch*, p 139.

53. Russell Taylor, *Hitch*, p 140.

54. Behlmar (ed), *Memo from David O Selznick*, p 252.

55. Spoto, *The Dark Side of Genius*, p 180.

56. Truffaut, *Hitchcock*, p 99.

57. Simon Callow, *Charles Laughton: A Difficult Actor* (Methuen, London: 1988) p 132.

58. Spoto, *The Dark Side of Genius*, p 188.

59. Behlmar (ed), *Memo from David O Selznick*, p 257.

60. Behlmar (ed), *Memo from David O Selznick*, p 258.

61. Truffaut, *Hitchcock*, p 104.

62. Behlmar (ed), *Memo from David O Selznick*, p 269.

63. Truffaut, *Hitchcock*, p 105.

64. Russell Taylor, *Hitch*, p 159.

65. Russell Taylor, *Hitch*, p 159.

66. Russell Taylor, *Hitch*, p 164.

67. Truffaut, *Hitchcock*, p 114.

68. Spoto, *The Dark Side of Genius*, p 237.

69. Gottlieb (ed), *Hitchcock on Hitchcock*, p 56.

70. Gary Morecambe and Martin Sterling, *Cary Grant: In Name Only* (Robson Books, London: 2001) p 136.

71. Gottlieb (ed), *Hitchcock on Hitchcock*, p 137.

72. Truffaut, *Hitchcock*, p 116.

73. Norman Lloyd, *Stages: Of Life in Theatre, Film and Television* (First Limelight, New York: 1993) p 71.

74. Lloyd, *Stages*, p 77.

75. Lloyd, *Stages*, pp 72–3.

76. Lloyd, *Stages*, p 73.

77. John Houseman, *Run-Through* (Simon & Schuster, New York: 1972) pp 479–80.

78. Truffaut, *Hitchcock*, p 125.

79. Joseph Cotten, *Vanity Will Get You Somewhere* (Columbus Books, London: 1987) p 63.

80. Spoto, *The Dark Side of Genius*, p 260.

81. Russell Taylor, *Hitch*, p 185

82. Cotten, *Vanity Will Get You Somewhere*, p 64.

83. Truffaut, *Hitchcock*, p 128.

84. Cotten, *Vanity Will Get You Somewhere*, p 67.

85. Gottlieb (ed), *Hitchcock on Hitchcock*, p 56.

86. Joel Finler, *Alfred Hitchcock: The Hollywood Years* (BT Batsford, London: 1992) p 60.

87. Condon and Sangster, *The Complete Hitchcock*, p 124.

88. Behlmar (ed), *Memo from David O Selznick*, p 342.

89. Behlmar (ed), *Memo from David O Selznick*, p 342.

90. Truffaut, *Hitchcock*, p 135.

91. Truffaut, *Hitchcock*, p 135.

92. Finler, *Alfred Hitchcock: The Hollywood Years*, p 63.

93. Russell Taylor, *Hitch*, p 195.

94. Behlmar (ed), *Memo from David O Selznick*, p 293.

95. Morecambe and Sterling, *Cary Grant: In Name Only*, p 167.

96. Spoto, *The Dark Side of Genius*, p 289.

97. Gottlieb (ed), *Hitchcock on Hitchcock*, p 56.

98. Truffaut, *Hitchcock*, p 143.

99. Behlmar (ed), *Memo from David O Selznick*, p 364.

100. Finler, *Alfred Hitchcock: The Hollywood Years*, p 73.

101. Truffaut, *Hitchcock*, p 148.

102. Gottlieb (ed), *Hitchcock on Hitchcock*, p 275.

103. Truffaut, *Hitchcock*, pp 148–9.

104. Donald Dewey, *James Stewart* (Turner Publishing, Atlanta: 1996), p 279.

105. Gottlieb (ed), *Hitchcock on Hitchcock*, p 276.

106. Gottlieb (ed), *Hitchcock on Hitchcock*, p 280.

107. Truffaut, *Hitchcock*, p 154.

108. Spoto, *The Dark Side of Genius*, p 310.

109. Justin Bowyer, *Conversations with Jack Cardiff* (BT Batsford, London: 2003) p 94.

110. Bowyer, *Conversations with Jack Cardiff*, p 95.

111. Truffaut, *Hitchcock*, p 158.

112. Maxford, *The A-Z of Hitchcock*, p 240.

113. Truffaut, *Hitchcock*, p 159.

114. Russell Taylor, *Hitch*, p 214.

115. Al Clark, *Raymond Chandler in Hollywood* (Proteus, London: 1982) p 104.

116. Clark, *Raymond Chandler in Hollywood*, p 106.

117. Clark, *Raymond Chandler in Hollywood*, p 107.

118. Truffaut, *Hitchcock*, p 162.

119. Clark, *Raymond Chandler in Hollywood*, p 111.

120. Truffaut, *Hitchcock*, p 165.

121. Barney Hoskyns, *Montgomery Clift: Beautiful Loser* (Bloomsbury, London: 1991) p 100.

122. Hoskyns, *Montgomery Clift*, p 101.

123. Hoskyns, *Montgomery Clift,* pp 101–2.

124. Truffaut, *Hitchcock*, p 168.

125. Truffaut, *Hitchcock*, p 168.

126. Truffaut, *Hitchcock*, p 171.

127. Gottlieb (ed), *Hitchcock on Hitchcock*, p 293.

128. Gottlieb (ed), *Hitchcock on Hitchcock*, p 96.

129. Gottlieb (ed), *Hitchcock on Hitchcock*, p 96.

130. Spoto, *The Dark Side of Genius*, p 343.

131. Spoto, *The Dark Side of Genius*, p 346.

132. Morecambe and Sterling, *Cary Grant: In Name Only*, p 199.

133. Steven DeRosa, *Writing with Hitchcock: The Collaboration of Alfred Hitchcock and John Michael Hayes* (Faber and Faber, London: 2001) p 120.

134. Truffaut, *Hitchcock*, p 190.

135. David Thomson, *The New Biographical Dictionary of Film: Fourth Edition* (Little Brown, London: 2002) p 464.

136. DeRosa, *Writing with Hitchcock*, p 128.

137. Gottlieb (ed), *Hitchcock on Hitchcock*, p 312.

138. DeRosa, *Writing with Hitchcock*, p 149.

139. DeRosa, *Writing with Hitchcock*, p 201.

140. Lloyd, *Stages*, p 174.

141. Truffaut, *Hitchcock*, p 203.

142. Truffaut, *Hitchcock*, p 204.

143. Spoto, *The Dark Side of Genius*, p 389.

144. Dewey, *James Stewart*, p 379.

145. Kim Novak interview with Anwar Brett in 1998.

146. Kim Novak interview with Anwar Brett in 1998.

147. Kim Novak interview with Anwar Brett in 1998.

148. Pat Hitchcock interview with Anwar Brett in 1998.

149. Finler, *Alfred Hitchcock: The Hollywood Years*, p 124.

150. Finler, *Alfred Hitchcock: The Hollywood Years*, p 125.

151. Pauline Kael, *Kiss Kiss Bang Bang* (Arena, London: 1970) p 318.

152. Richard Schickel, *Cary Grant: A Celebration* (Pavilion, London: 1983).

153. Gottlieb (ed), *Hitchcock on Hitchcock*, p 312.

154. Truffaut, *Hitchcock*, p 215.

155. Truffaut, *Hitchcock*, p 215.

156. Bill Krohn, *Hitchcock at Work* (Phaidon, London: 2000) p 217.

157. Alexander Walker, *Audrey: Her Real Story* (Weidenfeld & Nicolson, London 1994), p 169.

158. Maxford, *The A–Z of Alfred Hitchcock*, p 242.

159. Ronald Bergan, *Anthony Perkins: A Haunted Life* (Little Brown, London: 1995) p 145.

160. Bergan, *Anthony Perkins*, p 148.

161. Truffaut, *Hitchcock*, p 232.

162. Peter Bogdanovich on BBC Radio 4's 'Parker on Hitchcock' (2005).

163. Russell Taylor, *Hitch*, p 264.

164. David Freeman, *The Last Days of Alfred Hitchcock* (The Overlook Press, New York: 1984) p 7.

165. Evan Hunter, *Me and Hitch* (Faber and Faber, London: 1997) p 10.

166. Hunter, *Me and Hitch*, p 17.

167. Hunter, *Me and Hitch*, p 31.

168. Krohn, *Hitchcock at Work*, p 244.

169. Krohn, *Hitchcock at Work*, p 252.

170. Kael, *Kiss Kiss Bang Bang*, p 75.

171. Hunter, *Me and Hitch*, pp 75–6.

172. Truffaut, *Hitchcock*, p 253.

173. Daniel O'Brien, *Paul Newman* (Faber and Faber, London: 2004) p 120.

174. O'Brien, *Paul Newman*, p 121.

175. Lawrence J Quirk, *Paul Newman* (Taylor Publishing, Dallas: 1996) pp 146–7.

176. Bryan Forbes interviewed by the author 2005.

Filmography

As director, with date of release

Films

1927 *The Pleasure Garden.* With Virginia Valli, Carmelita Geraghy, Miles Mander, John Stuart.74 mins
The Mountain Eagle. With Bernhard Goetzke, John F Hamilton, Malcolm Keen, Nita Naldi. 68 mins
The Lodger. With Ivor Novello, June Tripp, Malcolm Keen, Marie Ault. 83 mins
Downhill. With Lilian Braithwaite, Ian Hunter, Ivor Novello, Robin Irvine. 74 mins
Easy Virtue. With Isabel Jeans, Franklin Dyall, Robin Irvine, Frank Elliott. 74 mins
The Ring. With Carl Brisson, Lillian Hall-Davis, Gordon Harker, Ian Hunter. 72 mins

1928 *The Farmer's Wife.* With Jameson Thomas, Lillian Hall-Davis, Gordon Harker, Gibb McLaughlin. 67 mins

1929 *The Manxman.* With Carl Brisson, Anny Ondra, Malcolm Keen, Randle Ayrton. 80 mins
Blackmail. With Anny Ondra, Sara Allgood, John Longden, Donald Calthrop. 78 mins

1930 *Elstree Calling*, co-directed by Andre Charlot, Jack Hulbert & Paul Murray. With Donald Calthrop, Gordon Harker, Tommy Handley, Anna May Wong. 95 mins

Juno and the Paycock. With Barry Fitzgerald, Maire O'Neill, Edward Chapman, Sara Allgood. 85 mins

Murder!. With Herbert Marshall, Norah Baring, Phyllis Konstam, Edward Chapman. 92 mins

1931 *The Skin Game*. With Edmund Gwenn, C V France, Helen Haye, Jill Esmond. 77 mins

1932 *Number Seventeen*. With Leon M Lion, Anne Grey, John Stuart, Donald Calthrop. 63 mins

Rich and Strange. With Henry Kendall, Joan Barry, Percy Marmont, Betty Amann. 83 mins

1933 *Waltzes from Vienna*. With Edmund Gwenn, Marcus Barron, Fay Compton, Frank Vosper. 80 mins

1934 *The Man Who Knew Too Much*. With Leslie Banks, Edna Best, Peter Lorre, Nova Pilbeam. 76 mins

1935 *The 39 Steps*. With Robert Donat, Madeleine Carroll, Godfrey Tearle, Lucie Mannheim. 81 mins

1936 *Secret Agent*. With John Gielgud, Madeleine Carroll, Peter Lorre, Robert Young. 86 mins

Sabotage. With Sylvia Sydney, Oscar Homolka, Desmond Tester, John Loder. 76 mins

1937 *Young and Innocent*. With Nova Pilbeam, Derrick De Marney, Percy Marmont, Edward Rigby. 82 mins

1938 *The Lady Vanishes*. With Michael Redgrave, Margaret Lockwood, Paul Lukas, Dame May Whitty. 97 mins

1939 *Jamaica Inn*. With Charles Laughton, Leslie Banks, Maureen O'Hara, Robert Newton. 108 mins

1940 *Rebecca*. With Laurence Olivier, Joan Fontaine, George

Sanders, Judith Anderson. 130 mins

Foreign Correspondent. With Joel McCrea, Laraine Day, Herbert Marshall, Albert Bassermann. 120 mins

1941 *Suspicion*. With Cary Grant, Joan Fontaine, Sir Cedric Hardwicke, Nigel Bruce. 99 mins

Mr and Mrs Smith. With Carole Lombard, Robert Montgomery, Gene Raymond, Jack Carson. 94 mins

1942 *Saboteur*. With Robert Cummings, Priscilla Lane, Otto Kruger, Norman Lloyd. 108 mins

1943 *Shadow of a Doubt*. With Joseph Cotten, Teresa Wright, MacDonald Carey, Henry Travers. 106 mins

1944 *Bon Voyage*. With John Blythe. 26 mins

Aventure Malgache. 31 mins

Lifeboat. With Tallulah Bankhead, William Bendix, Walter Slezak, John Hodiak. 96 mins

1945 *Spellbound*. With Ingrid Bergman, Gregory Peck, Michael Chekhov, Leo G Carroll. 111 mins

1946 *Notorious*. With Cary Grant, Ingrid Bergman, Claude Rains, Louis Calhern. 101 mins

1947 *The Paradine Case*. With Gregory Peck, Ann Todd, Alida Valli, Louis Jourdan. 125 mins

1948 *Rope*. With James Stewart, John Dall, Farley Granger, Sir Cedric Hardwicke. 80 mins

1949 *Under Capricorn*. With Ingrid Bergman, Joseph Cotten, Michael Wilding, Margaret Leighton. 117 mins

1950 *Stage Fright*. With Marlene Dietrich, Jane Wyman, Richard Todd, Michael Wilding. 110 mins

1951 *Strangers on a Train*. With Robert Walker, Farley Granger, Ruth Roman, Leo G Carroll. 100 mins

1953 *I Confess*. With Montgomery Clift, Anne Baxter, Karl Malden, O E Hasse. 95 mins

1954 *Dial M for Murder*. With Ray Milland, Grace Kelly, Robert Cummings, John Williams. 105 mins
Rear Window. With James Stewart, Grace Kelly, Wendell Corey, Raymond Burr. 113 mins

1955 *To Catch a Thief*. Cary Grant, Grace Kelly, Jessie Royce Landis, John Williams. 107 mins
The Trouble with Harry. With Edmund Gwenn, John Forsythe, Shirley MacLaine, Mildred Natwick. 100 mins

1956 *The Man Who Knew Too Much*. With James Stewart, Doris Day, Brenda De Banzie, Bernard Miles. 120 mins
The Wrong Man. With Henry Fonda, Vera Miles, Anthony Quayle, Harold Stone. 105 mins

1958 *Vertigo*. With James Stewart, Kim Novak, Barbara Bel Geddes, Tom Helmore. 128 mins

1959 *North by Northwest*. With Cary Grant, James Mason, Eva Marie Saint, Jessie Royce Landis. 136 mins

1960 *Psycho*. With Anthony Perkins, Janet Leigh, Vera Miles, John Gavin. 109 mins

1962 *The Birds*. With Tippi Hedren, Rod Taylor, Jessica Tandy, Suzanne Pleshette. 119 mins

1964 *Marnie*. With Tippi Hedren, Sean Connery, Diane Baker, Martin Gabel. 130 mins

1966 *Torn Curtain*. With Paul Newman, Julie Andrews, Lila Kedrova, Tamara Toumanova. 119 mins

1969 *Topaz*. With Frederick Stafford, Dany Robin, John Forsythe, John Vernon. 143 mins

1972 *Frenzy*. With Jon Finch, Barry Foster, Barbara Leigh-Hunt, Alec McCowen. 116 mins

1976 *Family Plot*. With Bruce Dern, Barbara Harris, William Devane, Karen Black. 121 mins

Television

'Alfred Hitchcock Presents'
First Season 1955–6
Revenge. With Vera Miles, Ralph Meeker, Ray Teal.
Breakdown. With Joseph Cotten, Raymond Bailey, Lane
Chandler.
The Case of Mr Pelham. With Tom Ewell, Raymond Bailey, Kay
Stewart.
Back for Christmas. With John Williams, Gavin Muir, Isobel
Elsom.

Second Season 1956–7
Wet Saturday. With Sir Cedric Hardwicke, John Williams,
Kathryn Givney.
Mr Blanchard's Secret. With Mary Scott, Robert Horton, Meg
Mundy
One More Mile to Go. With Norman Leavitt, David Wayne,
Louise Larrabee.

Third Season 1957–8
The Perfect Crime. With James Gregory, Vincent Price, John
Zaremba.
Lamb to the Slaughter. With Barbara Bel Geddes, Harold Stone,
Robert C Ross.
A Dip in the Pool. With Fay Wray, Keenan Wynn, Louise Platt.

Fourth Season 1958–9
Poison. With Arnold Moss, Wendell Corey, James Donald.
Banquo's Chair. With John Williams, Kenneth Haigh, Max
Adrian.

Fifth Season 1959–60
Arthur. With Patrick Macnee, Laurence Harvey, Hazel Court.
The Crystal Trench. With Patricia Owens, James Donald, Patrick
    Macnee.

Sixth Season 1960–1
Mrs Bixby and the Colonel's Coat. With Audrey Meadows, Les
    Tremayne, Stephen Chase
The Horse Player. With Claude Rains, Ed Gardner, Percy
    Helton.

Seventh Season 1961–2
Bang! You're Dead. With Billy Mumy, Marta Kristen, Biff
    Elliott.

'The Alfred Hitchcock Hour'
First Season 1962–3
I Saw the Whole Thing. With Kent Smith, John Forsythe, John
    Fiedler.

Bibliography

Baker, Roy Ward, *The Director's Cut* (Reynolds & Hearn, London: 2000).

Behlmer, Rudy (ed), *Memo from David O Selznick* (Viking Press, New York: 1972).

Bergan, Ronald, *Anthony Perkins: A Haunted Life* (Little Brown, London: 1995).

Bowyer, Justin, *Conversations with Jack Cardiff* (BT Batsford, London: 2003).

Callow, Simon, *Charles Laughton: A Difficult Actor* (Methuen, London: 1988).

Clark, Al, *Raymond Chandler in Hollywood* (Proteus, London: 1982).

Condon, Paul and Sangster, Jim, *The Complete Hitchcock* (Virgin, London: 1999).

Cotten, Joseph, *Vanity Will Get You Somewhere* (Columbus Books, London: 1987).

DeRosa, Steven, *Writing with Hitchcock: The Collaboration of Alfred Hitchcock and John Michael Hayes* (Faber and Faber, London: 2001).

Dewey, Donald, *James Stewart* (Turner Publishing, Atlanta: 1996).

Duncan, Paul, *Alfred Hitchcock: The Complete Films* (Taschen, Cologne: 2003).

Finler, Joel W, *Alfred Hitchcock: The Hollywood Years* (BT Batsford, London: 1992).

Freeman, David, *The Last Days of Alfred Hitchcock* (The Overlook Press, New York: 1984).

Gabler, Neil, *An Empire of Their Own: How the Jews Invented Hollywood* (WH Allen, London: 1988).

Gottlieb, Sidney (ed), *Hitchcock on Hitchcock* (Faber and Faber, London: 1997).

Hoskyns, Barney, *Montgomery Clift: Beautiful Loser* (Bloomsbury, London: 1991).

Houseman, John, *Run-Through* (Simon & Schuster, New York: 1972).

Hunter, Evan, *Me and Hitch* (Faber and Faber, London: 1997).

Kael, Pauline, *Kiss Kiss Bang Bang* (Arena, London: 1970).

Krohn, Bill, *Hitchcock at Work* (Phaidon, London: 2000).

Lloyd, Norman, *Stages: Of Life in Theatre, Film and Television* (First Limelight, New York: 1993).

MacLaine, Shirley, *My Lucky Stars: A Hollywood Memoir* (Bantam, London: 1995).

McGilligan, Patrick, *Fritz Lang* (Faber and Faber, London: 1997).

Maxford, Howard, *The A-Z of Hitchcock* (BT Batsford, London: 2002).

Mogg, Ken, *The Alfred Hitchcock Story* (Titan Books, London: 1999).

Morecambe, Gary and Sterling, Martin, *Cary Grant: In Name Only* (Robson Books, London: 2001).

Nourmand, Tony, and Wolff, Mark H (eds), *Hitchcock Poster Art* (Aurum Press, London,: 1999).

O'Brien, Daniel, *Paul Newman* (Faber and Faber, London: 2004).

Parker, John, *Sean Connery* (Victor Gollancz, London: 1993).

Parkinson, David (ed), *Mornings in the Dark: The Graham Greene Film Reader* (Carcanet, London: 1993).

Powell, Michael, *A Life in Movies: An Autobiography* (Faber and Faber, London: 2000).

Quirk, Lawrence J, *Paul Newman* (Taylor Publishing, Dallas: 1996).

Russell Taylor, John, *Hitch: The Life & Times of Alfred Hitchcock* (Plexus, London: 1994).

Schickel, Richard, *Cary Grant: A Celebration* (Pavilion, London: 1983).

Skaerved, Marlene Sheppard, *Dietrich* (Haus Publishing, London: 2003).

Spoto, Donald, *The Dark Side of Genius: The Life of Alfred Hitchcock* (Plexus, London: 1994).

Sweet, Matthew, *Shepperton Babylon* (Faber and Faber, London: 2005).

Thomson, David, *The New Biographical Dictionary of Film: Fourth Edition* (Little Brown, London: 2002).

Tims, Hilton, *Once a Wicked Lady* (Virgin Books, London: 1989).

Truffaut, François, *Hitchcock* (Secker & Warburg, London: 1968).

Walker, Alexander, *Audrey: Her Real Story* (Weidenfeld & Nicolson, London: 1994).

Warren, Patricia, *British Film Studios: An Illustrated History* (BT Batsford, London: 2001).

Index